Emilia Aylmer Blake

My only Love

Vol. I

Emilia Aylmer Blake

My only Love
Vol. I

ISBN/EAN: 9783337039851

Printed in Europe, USA, Canada, Australia, Japan

Cover: Foto ©ninafisch / pixelio.de

More available books at **www.hansebooks.com**

A Novel.

BY

EMILIA AYLMER BLAKE.

AUTHOR OF 'A CROWN FOR LOVE,' 'NELSON,' ETC.

IN THREE VOLUMES.

VOL. I.

οὐκ ἔστ ἐραστης ὅστις οὐκ ἀεὶ φιλεῖ

EURIPIDES.

' But this was taught me by the dove,
To die—and know no second love.
This lesson yet hath man to learn,
Taught by the thing he dares to spurn :
The bird that sings within the brake,
The swan that swims upon the lake,
One mate, and one alone, will take.'

BYRON.

London :

REMINGTON AND CO.,

133, NEW BOND STREET, W.

[*Removed from* 5, *Arundel Street, Strand.*]

1880.

CONTENTS OF VOL. I.

MY ONLY LOVE.

CHAPTER I.

SWEET SIXTEEN.

'Outre tous ces discours, toutes ces gentillesses
Ne vous faisait-il point aussi quelques caresses?

'Oh, tant ! Il me prenait et les mains et les bras,
Et de me les baiser il n'était jamais las.'

MOLIERE, Ecole des Femmes.

FAR away in old world Cornwall I was bred,
though not born, under the wing of a loving,
aged foster parent, my father's mother, a
widow, who cared but for me in the world.
No two companions ever were more
opposite than we, in tastes and fashions of

heart and mind, and yet I loved her well,
having no other truly to love.   Our home
was a neat house of modest pretensions,
in a marine town, which I shall call Stormouth, half fashionable in the 'season'
and occasionally galvanised into a show of
life by garrison balls and theatricals : but
we, my grannie and I, cared for none of
these things.   From childhood to girlhood
I had been acquainted with few even of
other children, but passed my time in such
solitary play as I could, until my grannie
got masters—the best the neighbourhood
could afford—to teach me all I was inclined
to learn ; and then I devoted myself to
study and hard work, being possessed with
a precocious ambition to do and to be
something under the sun which my poor
father and unknown mother closed their
eyes upon so early.

I was indeed an orphan, 'deprived of
light,' as the Greek origin of the word de-
rives it ; to live and die in the cold shadow
of the world's neglect, unless by some
means I could lift myself above it, and this
was early made known to me through my
grannie's frequent lament, 'What will be-

come of my poor child ? Bread and cheese I can give you,' she would say, ' but what is that to a girl like you ? Connection is everything, connection and position, and all our people are in their graves but you and I. How ever are you to marry ?'

That never troubled me ; but I took pleasure to read of the fair Gabrielle, how in a similar strait, a fortune-teller promised her higher destinies than those dues of her birth she was deprived of : upon me too, it was borne in by some prophetic instinct, that I should win a hero's heart, some Henri Quatre, whom heaven should make for me to be his wife, perhaps ; his love, assuredly ; his mistress ? no, never !

A cruel death fair Gabrielle died by poison. Ah, well ! that I might have braved. Since wishes were my only possessions, why should I not wish, like the wisest of the three sisters in the Eastern tale, to be the Caliph's wife, rather than his cook's or baker's ? and she had her wish ! Was I not, by my mother's side, a daughter of that wondrous land of the sun, where miracles are common as the light of noon ? My name, too, Leila ? Memories also I

had of a stately life in London, where my
father, the tenant for life of an inheritance
entailed in the male line, used to boast of
his little Indian beauty, his only child, and
say to other fathers, proud of their five, six,
or seven, 'I have eight in one.' He was
recalled to serve in India, and slain in
battle in the prime of manhood. He left
me an infant, not able yet to realise the
tremendous loss to be felt every hour of my
future life more and more keenly, but I
wept as much as a little child could weep
when they told me papa was gone away—
dead—and I begged to die too, and go to
him in heaven.

The crown without the cross! To that
I was not born. Happily the spirit of a
child is elastic as its tread, and will not
break under one blow. At thirteen I
began to feel as a woman, and often and
often would I walk alone by the sea,
making companions of the melancholy
waves, in mournful envy of other girls of
my age, whom I saw caressed and praised
by a fond father, while I had none to cling
to under heaven but the poor old grandmother, who rather reproved than en-

couraged my too demonstrative affection.
She had lived through too much to feel in
common with the young passionate heart
that chafed under her very kindness, and
hungered for other love than hers.

About this time it happened that a
name I had caught from my father's lips,
to be ever remembered with honor and
regard, rose very high in fame, and became common in every house throughout
England. I do not repeat it here, for
what cause will appear hereafter ; enough
that its great possessor passed one day in
our humble town, marking an epoch in the
annals of the same as surely as he fixed
the attention of every man, woman, child
and quadruped in the place. I too was
stirred by the hubbub and clatter of hoofs :
I marked him rising in his saddle while a
attendant orderly jogged, regulation wise,
with the brisk trot of his horse. I watched
the great man alight, measuring him with
my eyes—six feet of heroic manhood—my
father's height, and a presence not unlike
his. Something much more than a mortal,
though I felt that it would be a sin to give
way to my impulse—to fall down and wor-

ship him. Certainly, if no one could have
seen me, I should have liked to kiss the
particular spots on the ground where his
foot had rested. In all time to come I
could not choose but those worn out stone
steps must be inexpressibly dear to me for
his sake.

I partly forgot him, however, so far at
least as to waste no time in dreams, but returned with a fresh impulse to the task
which should fit me for that ' broad stream
of the world ' whose course attracted me.
It was discovered I had a voice. What
gentlemen value above all accomplishments
in a woman is to sing well, according to
my grandmother's lights, from which I
nowise dissented, but improved my gift to
the best of my power under the guidance
of the parish church organist, no mean
master, as my luck would have it, who
made me his pet pupil. But with all this,
I yet craved beauty, fearing much lest in
that I should not keep the promise of my
childhood. Was I plain or pretty ? Alas !
I could not resolve that question to my
satisfaction, neither by the aid of my glass,
nor yet by means of the booby-like conduct

of my old master's nephew, an ingenuous
youth three years older than myself, whom
I had used as my slave from the respective
ages of seven and ten, making him useful
in stitching my doll's clothes, and, later on,
as an errand boy between me and his uncle,
until, having completed his sixteenth year,
he adopted an odd fashion of blushing
through all his pimples as red as a poppy
at sight of me, and, if he happened to find
me alone in our parlour, making his way
out again, with a stammering apology, as
fast as his long legs could carry him. Out
of such demeanour on the part of my old
playmate I could make no sense, but, con-
vulsed with laughter, would describe the
scene to his uncle, whose—' I've heard tell
of you, Miss Lily' was always provocative
of a fresh peal of merriment from me.
The old man was very fond of me, and
took these vagaries as if they were hurts
to something belonging to himself. The
nephew was too young, the uncle at sixty
too old to fall in love, I foolishly thought.
I knew nothing yet of men and their
ways.

And now I touched upon sixteen ! Living

shut up in the proverbial band-box, which, in due course, goes on to the shelf, but wherein, as unenterprising mammas assure their discontented daughters, their 'luck will come' to them as soon as in any Belgravian drawing room ; and there did fate very nearly find me out, sooth to say, in the unlovely, but substantial shape of a new candidate for our Borough of Stormouth, a lacker of advancement, matrimonial as well as political. His lady mother and canvasser-in-chief waited, according to form, upon my grandmother, to make request for her small influence, she having some property in and about the town. My grandmother was not too gracious, being an oldfashioned Tory of staunch principles, in contradistinction to the new candidate, who went in as a *dilettante* Radical, or 'Moderate Liberal,' as dame Mauleverer, his mother, put it euphuistically to grannie. 'I don't understand these distinctions,' observed the latter, with much simplicity ; ' but is not Mr. Mauleverer a high Tory ? I should think he must be, the name is so good.'

'Well, not quite what you would call a

Tory ; in fact, there is no such thing in
the world now ; a gentleman must be
liberal and make his way with all classes,
high and low, or he'll soon be thrust out
of his place. But my son's principles are
the same as yours and mine, my dear
friend, only he must act in opposition to
the Government and make himself trouble-
some. That's the way to get into power
now-a-days. He must compel them to take
him into the Privy Council to keep him
quiet.'

' I'm sorry for it ; that used not to be
the way with honourable men. I'm afraid
the whole of England is rotten to the
core.'

' That it is, my dear madam ; all everyone of us has to do is to cut out our own
slice outside the general corruption—to
keep clear of it, in fact. I shall be happy
to do anything within my power for you
and your little grand-daughter. Of course
you'll give all your interest to my son ?'

' Well—yes ; at least, I'll think about it,'
hesitated grannie, and at this stage of the
proceedings I made my entrance on the
scene. I had just come in from bathing,

with dripping hair, and toilette—such as it was—demolished by the wind. Mrs. Mauleverer looked down at my feet, and then at my head, from a height of contempt that conjured up from my hurt self-esteem a very demon of rebellion. There was a defiance in the courtsey I dropped down to the ground, to show I knew how to do it, as my grandmother introduced me. 'Young girls ought to be taught how to dress,' predicated my enemy of me ; ' or otherwise they know no better than to make frights of themselves, and no one can tell what they may lose by giving a bad impression. That child has a great look of her father. Ah ! I knew him very well. Yes, she has a look of him, but his complexion was nothing like so dark ; he was a fine handsome Englishman.'

' I have heard I have my mother's complexion,' I remonstrated.

'Oh no, oh no ! not at all ; she was a very beautiful woman. And now I must take myself off, I have so many to call upon. I make sure I can reckon upon you, dear Mrs. Fortescue, and as for that little minx, she may make a great match yet ;

dress her, dress her!' My grandmother, neither pledging herself, nor yet demurring to any of Mrs. Mauleverer's conclusions, that lady, as it were to clinch her argument, stepped back into the room to say —'My son shall call on you himself,' and with that left us, my grandmother half-flattered, myself wholly indignant at her impertinence, meant for condescension. One thing she had made sensible to me in her praise of my parents, that I was by comparison to be despised in her eyes, and to this, I made up my mind, her son should be no party, good luck and bright wit favouring me; so I followed the enemy's good counsel, and dressed myself for conquest, crowning the achievement by a most mischievous hat of my own device. Mr. George Augustus Mauleverer came, saw, and was overcome; so true is it that the masculine disposition is to be subdued by a bit of straw and a tuft of feather.

I lay in wait for him in the garden in front of our house, pretending not to expect, or know him when he came; and by this *ruse de guerre* quite threw him off his pedestal as a man of family and fashion. At first sight of me he gave a start of surprise, doubtless to find me so opposite to the dusky, dwarfish fright I had been described to him. Not content with this satisfaction, I drew him on, after he followed me into my grandmother's drawing-room, into something very like serious admiration ; ignorant as I was, yet all the more wise with the cunning in such matters, which, old Montaigne says, comes by nature as the gift of the author of all evil to every daughter of Eve, however young and simple she may be.

Next day, while unconscious of the amount of mischief I had achieved, and ruminating on its possible extent with some alarm, I was aroused by the mother of my victim sweeping down like a provoked kite upon our dove-cot. With much ostentation of mystery, and the initiation of my grand-mother into a mighty secret, she ordered ' the little goose,' meaning my too quick-witted self, out of the room. What she there and then imparted in most solemn confidence to my grandmother I failed not to coax out, word for word, after she was gone, nor shall I by concealing the same run risk of crossing any reader's feminine curiosity, or masculine rather, compared to which latter our weaker faculty is but ' as water unto wine.'

In one word I had made a conquest of George Augustus Mauleverer, so that his five thousand a year, prospective title of M.P., and somewhat stumpy person were metaphorically placed at my small feet, always provided that I, by fortune, birth, and connection, could make some decent show of equivalent. This was not to be calculated too rigidly, inasmuch as George had his fancy to please : he might easily marry a girl in his own class of life, she, little minx, for her part, might make a higher match, though that was most improbable; but those two young people would never be so happy as by uniting themselves for life. How old was the chit ? Not sixteen. Why, they say she's seventeen all out—quite old enough to be married when a gentleman is willing to have her. Wait ? No, George Augustus would not wait. It would be an impertinence to ask a gentleman to wait.

Five thousand pounds! Not enough to pay election expenses. No matter: another five thousand on death of grand-mother. Very well; five hundred a year should be settled on her, if she survived her husband. But the estate? Oh no! George Augustus would not settle the estate. She might die without a son, and he would have to marry again. Was she not consumptive?

All reflections made, I jumped to the conclusion that if anybody was to be con-stituted match-maker in my behoof, Mrs. Mauleverer was the very last person in the world whose interference I would suffer, while poor grannie proved herself a mere feather to be twisted about the shrewd dowager's thick fingers.

'I won't have him,' I blurted out, to dear old grannie's consternation.

'Why, my dear Lily, how can you say so? And why? Tell me why.'

'Why, because I won't, and I don't care for him, and I never can, and there's an end of it.'

'Why, you seemed to like him so much yourself.'

' Like to torment him, you mean.'

'Oh, Lily!'

' Well, like him in a way, but not to marry him.'

'You'll never see such a match again if you miss him ; you must marry some time.'

' Well, perhaps not.'

'My dear, but you must; I would have you marry a duke, if I could.'

' And because you cannot, I'm to take the first that comes, whether I like him or not.'

' You'll grow to like him if you marry him ; you may as well like him as anyone else.'

' I don't see that. He's a little tubby figure ; and you know you brought me up to admire height in a man. My father was six feet high,' I pouted in deprecation.

' As if I could foresee a man of such a position would propose, and you want to refuse him for that.'

' Well, and his politics—a Whig and a Radical. When I was a child, you warned me against even dancing with any man who was not a Tory, and now you want me to marry in the teeth of your own principles.'

' Women's principles, my love, must give

way to paramount necessity ; think of the
danger of your being left an old maid.'

At that I laughed a long and merry
laugh, ringing with the bright scorn of sixteen summers.

'Ah, I can see no good to come of this,'
she feebly remonstrated, and on a renewal
of confabulation, between both old ladies,
it was decided that George Augustus
should speak for himself, who, no doubt,
all important preliminaries being once
satisfactorily arranged, would easily overcome the forgotten trifle of my opposition.
Accordingly George Augustus came at his
leisure, a few days afterwards, to do what
he should have done at first—make love
to me.

It was the first formal declaration I had
ever received from a man, but after the
first blush—(literally), which for a moment
tinged my cheek — not apt to color
hitherto, the more he prayed and pressed
the more indifferent I felt, the more ardent
he for my coldness. I could have looked
him quietly in the face through it all, and
only dropped my eyelids because I thought
it was the proper thing to do. It had been

enjoined upon me not to be rude to him, to let him kiss my hand; and so much did he abuse this permission that I doubt whether the Queen's hand, in all her life, received a like quantity of kisses to mine, in that one long summer's day.

The first taste of love was sweet to me, if not the lover. While his lips pressed my fingers, and crept up the tiny wrist to print themselves upon the soft smoothness of the rounded arm, I wandered away in imagination towards that other, once seen and now recalled to memory, and thought in envy of the happy woman who should win from him such delicate, tender caresses. He was not married! That flashed upon me; and should I marry now? I broke away from the profaning touch, resolved to suffer it no more.

This was no longer a matter of choice with me, having provoked my assailant too far.

'Lily, my darling, listen to me like a darling,' he remonstrated; 'say three little words—" I love you," or if you cannot, one kiss.'

Before I could struggle he had done it.

Angered and ashamed I began to cry.
It was the first kiss I had ever had from a
man, except once when I was four years
old.   A painter to whom I sat with my
father for our portraits called me 'little
Chatterbox;'   I,   not   understanding   the
epithet, asked for an explanation, and received a kiss which I, desiring to return
with a decorous slap in the face, mounted
upon a footstool with that intent, but found
I could not by at least a couple of feet
reach up to my purpose.   Vexed at this,
I burst into tears, and the like did now.

'Oh, Lily, Lily, your beautiful eyes—
don't spoil them like that.   I'll kiss away
those tears for you, naughty girl!   I won't
be put away.   Why, have I pulled down
your hair, and you want to put it up again
with your little fingers ?   What a heap of
lovely hair—all fallen down! oh, you poor
little thing!'

He did not tell me I was beautiful, but
his looks flattered me the more that his
tongue was reticent.   My eyes, I knew,
were something remarkable ; nurses and
maids from my earliest years having
worried me on the subject.   My hair, dark

with glints of red, was at least rare in tint
and luxuriance. George Augustus looked
and looked, as if he would devour and
swallow me up—little hands, great eyes,
hair and all.

Then I was fair! Sweet it was to be
taught that lesson. To be assured I had
so much to enrich the eyes, and captivate
the heart which should satisfy the love-
thirst that grew upon me : but this was not
the man. The more he pleaded the more
obstinately I put away the deep draught of
passion thus thrust upon me in the ugly
glass wherefrom I so coyly refused to sip.
Why did I so ? Woman seldom does re-
ject love that is true. He should have
persevered, and then he might have won
me, and enjoyed his fancy; I might have
lived to content the world—if not myself
—a happy woman without a history, and
not now be tracing these remorseful lines.
Again and again he pleaded with me,
'Lily, I am afraid I cannot make you love
me,' and got no answer but—'I cannot
tell; I don't know—wait until I see you
again,' and, with that cold comfort, he
started for London, on business, I was told.

I did not believe it, but gave way to a horrible suspicion, which rose upon me out of some scattered phrases of his. It so happened that some days before, a celebrated singer, Mrs. Forest, had made her appearance at Stormouth, and I, being myself an amateur musician of lofty aspirations, made a point of hearing the famous prima donna. As a woman she bore an evil name, having made a conquest, on the stage, of a poor lord who suffered her to remain in the path of temptation until she ran away with one of her professional coadjutors, and, being divorced from her noble husband, married him. The story was noised that she was no more faithful to her present than to her former vows, and certain it was that George Augustus was an enthusiastic admirer of her beauty, both of face and voice. The local Mrs. Grundy was careful to make me aware of the fact that his praises of Mrs. Forest were such as a gentleman should not bestow on one lady, while paying his addresses to another.

A council upon my perversity was held forthwith between Mrs. Mauleverer and

my grandmother, and thereupon I was
strenuously urged by the latter to give my
reasons. Thus pushed, I gave conjectures
instead, to the effect that I was convinced
George Augustus had gone away on no
business, but some love affair—some objectionable love affair—most likely Mrs.
Forest had to do with it. This I charged
grannie not to repeat after me, but she
did so at once to Mrs. Mauleverer, who,
shocked beyond measure, repeated to her
son, the next time he came down, every
word I had said. He, to make the case
worse, denied nothing, but laughed with
right good glee, and said, ' Is it too much
gallantry I am accused of ?' Horror of
horrors ! I had stumbled upon the truth,
though how I did so is as great an enigma
to myself as it was to the two lady mothers.
At my guilty adorer I could scarcely look
for very shame. Something else George
Augustus had done in London besides
make love where he should not ; he had
played and lost several thousand pounds, to
be promptly discharged as a debt of honor,
while legal difficulties hindered the raising
of the sum by mortgage of his estates.

The result was, George Augustus must
have forthwith either my five thousand
pounds, or another woman's, in the honorable way of marriage, which could not,
therefore, be postponed. His mother had
found a girl answering all requirements for
his wife with four times the sum. So it
was put to me at once to say 'Yea or nay;'
and I still denied him during a nine hours'
siege, from three in the afternoon until two
hours past midnight—but I was new to the
world, and from such a manner of wooing
I revolted. All was vain, and he went
away sorrowful, to seek a more complaint,
wealthier bride.

That was over, but not the consequences; my home had no longer the
negative merit of quiet. I had offended
against all family law, tradition and pre-
cedent, and baulked poor grannie of the
eager desire of her life, to see me married
early. I had had my chance, and thrown
it away, and never could such another be
looked for again, if I lived a hundred
years. To this Mrs. Grundy failed not
to chime in with a thousand 'aye, ayes,'
and added that I was dangerous moreover,

a girl likely to do much mischief and no good.

My old music-master's wife was among the first to propound this view of my adventure, provoked by her husband with symptoms of something very like jealousy on my account. One day, at my grand-mother's request, I was preparing some election streamers with Mr. Mauleverer's colours—of course, when he was still a bachelor. The couple surprised me at my task, and while by the wife I was com-mended therefore, the husband gave vent to grumbles of disapprobation of my making too much of the Whig candidate.

'What has turned you politician all of a sudden?' shrewdly threw in the lady. 'I never thought you had found out the difference between Whig and Tory before.' Then, turning to her husband, 'Perhaps you think Miss Fortescue ought to choose her husband by the color of his coat.'

Thus challenged, the organist's temper broke into a discordant key. I too, much disconcerted, let fall the compromising, gaudy-coloured shreds and patches, which he, snatching up, tore into smaller divisions flung into the grate, and exclaimed ; ‘ What does she want to marry for ?—whims of women !’ Two words comprised the wife’s comment on this outburst—‘ Old fox !’ she cried, with the accompaniment of a box on the ear such as sent the peccant organist spinning round on his chair (an easy one on castors), and knocked him against the chimney-piece by the neat impetus of the blow, the lady’s hand being small for the result she achieved. He bore it like a lamb, and, without one word of justification, lay quietly under the ‘ soft impeachment.’

Next time I had a singing lesson I was made acquainted with my master’s household tribulations in my behoof. His wife, much displeased at his too great partiality for me as his pet pupil, had put thereon the most objectionable construction, scolding him so perpetually as to give him no peace by day or night. ‘ She’s the same as a daughter to you, but with a difference, Mr. Nightingale—with a difference! Now, don’t you contradict me in that. If I were to die to-morrow, you’d make her an offer next day.’ This he repeated to me with the comment that women's eyes have most extraordinary powers of discernment ; and at last, from being wrongfully suspected of making love to me, and constantly provoked by the false charge, he began to make it true, to my great discomfort, the more so that I was fond of the old man, and had long valued his harmless predilection as the most pleasant friendship I had yet known. I would have kept it thus, had it been left to me ; but this, jealousy crept in and forbade.

To aggravate the hardship, I had just begun with him the study of a new opera, on mastering which I had set my whole heart, and a hard task I had to achieve my object and keep my teacher in decorous order. '_Quis custodes custodiet ?_' was the problem I had to solve, and did so with tolerable harmony, considering the difficulties. When my last lesson was over I gave a loud sigh of relief, to which my master responded with a queer little moan, and told me, though I sang with such divine expression, he could tell I had got no heart.

'Why do you say that ?' I asked ; 'is it

because I don't care about George Mauleverer?'

'You don't care for any man on earth, but you're the most cruel little coquette alive,' responded my censor.

'Coquette? Why am I a coquette?'

'You want to sing better than any girl in England.'

'Well, and suppose I do?'

'Merely for the sake of entrapping more victims—all female vanity. Your face brightens up when you've produced a fine note, as another's would when her lover had kissed her.'

'Oh, you malicious old thing!'

'You've got no heart for an old man, anyhow; I know you don't care a pin about me, except for what I can teach you.'

'Oh, but I do.'

'No, you don't. Why now, I've gone through the whole of this part with you, day after day, and after all my trouble I've never had a kiss of you yet.'

'Well, you may kiss my hand, if you like.' He did so, rather elaborately, and, saying, 'I'm an old man, Miss Lily,' was fain not to stop at that.

'Oh, I can't allow you—indeed I can't, after what you told me Mrs. Nightingale said, although I don't believe a word of it of you.'

'Mrs. Nightingale be blessed! What does she know about our business together?'

'Oh, but she thinks she does, and I must not allow you.'

'Ah, well, you're a singular being—no feeling at all, no more than the keys of the piano,' he murmured, dolefully; then added, 'Somebody will play upon you some day; I'm an old fool to love you, but I do.'

'Oh, but not in the way Mrs. Nightingale thinks.'

'Oh, women have sharp eyes. She has; but you—you won't see it, that's all.'

'Why, what can I possibly do? You've got a wife already, you know.'

This was unanswerable, but he sulked all the rest of the afternoon.

Mrs. Nightingale was not blind to the state of affairs, although I kept honorably silent. I hold a lady bound to repel any vagaries of fancy towards herself on the part of another lady's husband, but not to tell of him, it being not to be expected that a girl can go fighting her way through the world; if she cannot take care of herself without becoming an apple of discord between man and wife, I take it she lacks either common sense or true womanly dignity. Safe I was, except from gossip, and this, whispering in my grandmother's ear, brought my singing lessons to an abrupt stop, in full *crescendo* of progress in the art, to my intense mortification.

I became sick and weary exceedingly of the good town of Stormouth, where I was not allowed to have a friend, where no pursuit could be tolerated in a young lady but the 'weary, stale, flat, and unprofitable' one of husband hunting, as many and many an overbold spinster of the evil-thinking locality had proved that chase to be before my time.

CHAPTER II.

THE GOD OF MY IDOLATRY.

'However marr'd, of more than twice her years,
Seamed with an ancient sword-cut on the cheek,
And bruised and bronzed, she lifted up her eyes
And loved him with that love which was her doom.'

TENNYSON : *Elaine.*

SHORTLY after these annoyances, an incident befel to disturb the placidity of the
Stormouth regions, like a great stone
thrown into a mill-pond, troubling muddy
waters that have been wont to stagnate in
peace and quietness : no less an event than
the arrival of my hero at the neighbouring
seat of the noble viscount who took his
title from the town, heralded by magnificent
preparations for balls, theatricals, fireworks,
and hubbub of every kind, to welcome the
great man whom 'all England delighted to

honor,' as the worthy mayor stated in his
address, delivered in new robes, made
expressly for the occasion, as were those of
the throng in silk and muslin, who did
their worst to make the man believe himself lord and master of all womankind,
having but to stoop to any one of the
many conquests thrust upon him.   There
was to be a county ball in the town, to
which my grandmother and I, by right of
birth, had access, although we had never as
yet made the attempt to hold our own in
that respect among the local society.   It
was to be my first appearance in the world,
and, grannie was confident, to result in a
blaze of triumph.   She said I must be the
belle of the ball, and quash and put down,
by my presence and attractions, any
malicious attempts to keep me out of my
natural sphere by jealous women.   Her
own case, when a girl, had been identical.
She was considered plain by her own sex,
certainly never acknowledged as a beauty
until the men cried her up as such ; and
now it was my time to meet the same good
fortune.

'I cannot take you out like girls who

have young mothers,' she said ; 'my day
is gone by for that, but I'll do all I can for
you, my love. This is your best chance ;
make the most of it. I shall make myself
known to the great man. He was a firm
friend of your father, and if he notices you,
it will make your position in the county ;
so, remember, between every dance you
must come back to me.'

There was little need for this last
caution, for, to my bitter surprise and
shame, I sat by the wall, dance after dance,
by my grandmother's side, unsought for by
any man. All the half-bred young men
about the town, whom at one time or
another I had snubbed, took their revenge
now, looked at me, and passed me by,
pretending not to see me, as I had done to
them in the street. Even Mr. Nightingale's nephew, who would have liked to
dance with me, lacked pluck to single
himself out from the rest by offering the
attention. In no place that I know of so
much as at a ball is the situation so
mastered by the very pettiest specimens
of the lords of creation. I saw obscure
squirelings and puny curates twirling about

magnificent damsels of twice my propor-
tions, jogging and butting out of all time
for want of knowing better, not, as of late
the fashion, because it is 'the thing' to
dance in defiance of measure, a custom my
tuneful ear and deft feet could never
habituate themselves to.

One militia captain, whom I reckoned
among my few friends, being, though a
married man, a great dancer, contrived,
with surpassing skill and agility, to spin
round half a score of heavy matrons, one
after the other, the average circumference
of whose waists I calculated at four feet,
the diameter of the same being at least
sixteen inches, while their round, fat faces
beamed with delight at the long-unac-
customed gallantry. On poor me the
provoking captain never threw his eyes,
and I had to rest content perforce with the
cold comfort of knowing myself the best
dancer in the room, doomed to wall-
flowerdom at sixteen!

Was it my dress that was in fault, or my
rebellious hair, that knew no pomade nor
curling iron to curb its clustering heaps?
As to costume, I had done my best

according to my lights: I was attired in clouds of white gauze and blonde, draped with a scarf from my native land, of the 'woven air' of Decca's looms—a stream of gold and crimson, while roses of the like colour formed a coronal round my head, and a few diamonds sparkled on my neck and bosom. I heard a whisper—'eccentric'—as I took my place in the room. It was plain the women were against me as a possible rival, the men quiescent through worldly respect for the female leaders of society.

I sat in silent though vile durance until past one o'clock. I was sick to get away, but our carriage was ordered at two, and it would not do to make a noise and attract any more observation than we could avoid. For nearly three hours we had sat, no one offering to take us into the supper room, until we spontaneously made a move in that direction, when our deserted side of the room made us more conspicuous in remaining there than in a voyage of discovery through the crowd. Borne onward with the stream, my grandmother first, we were parted in mid-current through

the obstacle of a doorway, where she stuck
between two ponderous dowagers, whose
equal rank forbade either to give way,
while together they could not shoot the
narrow passage without damaging each
other as well as any unlucky lighter craft
wedged in between ; while I, caught in the
increasing block behind, could by no means
render poor grannie any assistance. Un-
accustomed for many years to the crush of
a high-class mob, she cried to me in alarm,
and drew the general attention upon her
distress. It so chanced that the hero of
the night stood, surrounded by a bevy of
fair worshippers, a few steps from the
struggle, safe beyond, in smooth waters
beneath the reserved daïs in the supper
room, sacred to the ladies patronesses. His
quick eye took in the situation, and almost
before they were aware, he slid cunningly
from amidst the female coil that hemmed
him in, and, in half a moment, extricated
the old lady from her trouble, without
offence to her oppressors, such masterful
good breeding and tact surrounded the
man. As she got through, I followed,
making a dart after her through the open-

ing, and his eye fell upon me, standing by her side.

'Your daughter?' he said, inquiringly.

'My grandchild. I may say, my daughter. The only child of my son, who is dead; you knew him—Colonel Fortescue.'

'Colonel Fortescue! the most rising man in India when he was killed! Then you were his mother. How wonderful to meet you like this! Have I not seen you before?'

'Yes. I kept house with my son in London some years before his death. You dined with us several times before you were so great a hero as you are now'—she added, smiling, 'I am not surprised that I should have gone quite out of your memory.'

'I do remember you then, one of the finest women in London still: your fame as a beauty only beginning to give place to your son's as a soldier.'

'We will not talk of my beauty now. Age and grief have made a change—all, all gone,' and she shook her head mournfully.

'We cannot say that, who see you so accompanied, though mademoiselle is not in the least like you.'

'She is like her father.'

'Yes, I see the resemblance—a face to win upon one. She is pretty, very pretty; not a dazzling beauty though, like yours.'

'Ah, I am an old woman, and a very sorrowful one. She is all my beauty now.'

'Well, you are happy in her. Is not that so?' He appealed to me.

I looked in his face to read my destiny there before I made reply. Happy I had not been hitherto, since I felt a woman's heart throb into life beneath my scarce budding breast; but before me opened the possibilities of Paradise, set within those eyes of his, bent down upon me in their tender hazel light, with a smile of inexpressible sweetness, such as in man or woman I never saw before, so witching in its modest sympathy. Though worn with war, and, like Othello's, 'declined in the vale of years,' the lordly beauty of his face and form was beyond comparison with any human being I had ever looked upon—or so it seemed to me. I trembled, utterly lost, and could not speak until I drew my gaze from beneath the light that fascinated me, not knowing what I did, but anyhow I would not speak false to him.

'I have never been happy,' I murmured, hopelessly, 'since my father died; he was very fond of me. I do not expect to be happy ever again.'

'Not happy, you? That would be folly. I wish I were as happy as you—as young, as bright, as gifted. Oh! I am old and worn out in comparison.'

'What matter, when you have saved your country? saved us all? I would give my life to do as much.'

'Beautiful young enthusiast! No; keep your life; it will be very dear to somebody some day.'

His rich voice fell with these last words; it was clear and true as a bell, but deeper than any metal could vibrate, softest in the lower tones. I did not hear—I felt it thrill through and through my veins, with an indescribable effect, such as the chords of a harp have upon me, but immeasurably

stronger. There was no longer any re-
sistance in me ; I had met my fate ; I gave
one little cry, 'Oh, shall I ever see you
again ?'

'I am not going away to-night for ever ;
I'll call to-morrow and pay my respects to
Mrs. Fortescue. We must have her quite
well after the shock to her nerves to-
night. You will go home soon ? You do
not care for dancing ?'

'Not any more now,' I said, ashamed to
own I had not danced at all. He did not
dance and that was enough. If he must
quit me for those women of rank, he would
not dance with them ; therefore as he could
pay me no more attention, I was content to
go. It was a great and wonderful thing
that I should see him in our own house
to-morrow.

He did not keep his word so soon, but
redeemed it three days afterwards, when I
had given him up, as the only relief from
hour upon hour of suspense and anguish.
I was sitting with my harp in my embrace,
trying to sing away a little of my pain ;
my grandmother, too, after three days of
mortifying disappointment, declared we

were not of consequence enough for so great
a man to keep his promise to us, and, growing bitter at the slight, forbade any more
preparation to receive him, so that when he
did come—no longer expected—she was
out of the way, and he surprised me alone.
It may well be imagined I lost all self-
possession, a girl so utterly unused to the
world thus taken at disadvantage. In a
moment he relieved my embarrassment,
saying—

'Forgive me—I should not have stolen
in like a thief; I was listening to your
voice outside your window. I never heard
anything like it, in such a young creature
too! What was it you sang?'

Here I blushed anew, more overcome
than ever. The song was a love lament I
had read in an old book. The melody had
come to me in thinking of him; I could
not tell him this: I dared not answer him.

'Can you show me the music?' he inquired. 'These simple airs that go to the
heart are a great weakness of mine. You
sang it so feelingly! Perhaps you have
not the music?'

'I have not. I do not know that it is

written; I could not tell how it came to
me; I have never learnt it.'

'You composed it yourself, perhaps?'

'I don't know that I ever composed anything. Don't you say so, pray!' I pleaded,
with tingling cheeks, detected in my guilt.

'Nay, 'tis your own, What a young
genius you are! What a gift to make happiness around you!'

'I wish I could, but that is a fairy's
privilege, not a mortal's.'

'Well, you are a fairy; you are not like
any girl I ever saw. I seem to see a wide
space dividing your home from the whole
world without. How can you be otherwise
than happy?'

'I should be happy if I could see you—
for half an hour once in every fortnight.'

Too artlessly I made reply; he smiled
tenderly, but with a little wonder mingling
with his content; he perceived, what I
knew not yet, his conquest of me: I had
betrayed that secret, which, unasked, unsought, no woman ever gave up to man
and repented not. I was a fool.

Not such a fool, either, but that I had a
shadow of reason to disguise my folly;

my attraction for him was as strong as his admiration was genuine and sincere; had it been otherwise, had my imagination only been in fault, I had deserved no sympathy, no, not even pity, to have yielded my heart up for a few sweet words!

'You ought to come out in London,' he went on; 'I come so seldom to this part of the country; but if we meet seldom, we can correspond: I shall be so proud of your friendship! You will write to me?'

'If you wish. You must make my grandmother give me leave; she has such a horror of girls writing to gentlemen, but to you, it is not the same as to anyone else."

'My dear child, I am old enough to be your father. Leila—is not that your name? may I call you Leila? You don't want to be Miss Fortescue to me?'

'Anything you like—anything in the world. Is there any girl in England could refuse you anything?' I answered in extenuation, simple wax as I was in his hands.

'Then I shall call you Leila; 'tis a lovely name.'

'I have often been tormented about it; they say it has a strange, barbarian sound.'

'Do they? the idiots!'

'You have heard it before, being in India?'

'Heard it! who has not heard of Meignoun and Leila, the Romeo and Juliet of the East? I must translate the poem to you some day; 'twas that made Hafiz famous—the oriental Byron.'

'I am glad my name is Leila—'twas my mother's too.'

'Leila—and what will you call me, between ourselves? I hate titles and surnames among intimate friends.'

'How do you wish me to call you?'

He had all but said, 'My love;' he checked himself, and thought before he replied, 'I have three Christian names: choose which you like best, and call me that, when we are by ourselves together, and when you write to me.'

He gave me three to choose from, 'Arthur' was one; being that he never used in public, I seemed to like it best, as it should be peculiar to me, sacred to our affection : 'twas a name familiar to me from a child, being bred in the West Country, the native soil of the hero-king, the antitype of him I had now the great happiness to love. I said, 'As you wish it—you shall be King Arthur to me.'

He took the gentle flattery as it came, warm from my heart ; his name be henceforth Arthur to you, my reader, as to me. I would not reveal to you who he was to the world, telling you this 'ower true' story ; his identity you shall never know, never guess, while calling him by that other name, emblazoned in the world's history, among the few in our days who shall be added to the short roll-call of England's greatest. Let not the faintest shadow of a taint be cast on that, for any poor sorrows of mine. My part is to bear these in silence, for the sake of that whereon I had set my pride.

All this being concluded between us before my grandmother entered on the scene, upon her so doing, Arthur's manner took an entire change to mere frank kindness, such as a man of fine feeling, gentle to all, will specially show to a woman

advanced in years, and an old friend.
Her very dog, a spoiled pet, who hated
strangers, made advances to him, won
caresses from him, and from me deep envy.
Truly, he was kind and tender to every
living thing ; never could he be otherwise
to me, a young girl so fond of him.

He gave good reasons for his delay in
calling, being not altogether master of his
time with his host Lord Stormouth, and
inquired if we knew him ? A mortifying
question, as we did not, though all the
world did in our county. It was best to tell
the truth in the mildest form ; I had never
been 'out' at all, and grandmother, after
twenty years' absence, returned to her own
county almost a stranger ; it was nobody's
business to set a girl like me in the place
to which by old descent I was entitled,
and less than this I would not accept from
society. I dared not quite say so much
before my grandmother, but I said enough
for him to divine what I wished to convey.
Taking in the whole situation, he addressed
himself to her, and said :

'Your granddaughter would be an orna-
ment to any court, if she were known.

London is the place where she would be admired; you intend to bring her out there, do you not?'

'I am not rich enough to live in London according to our station, as we did in my son's time; poor Leila is but a country girl, I fear, for the rest of her life; unless she will marry a husband who will show her off in town, which it is her own fault she has not done already.'

He smiled delight and said:

'Hard to please, eh? You must not blame her for that; who should be, if she were not? The man will come!' and he added, so low that I alone could hear, 'the happiest man in the whole world.'

'Well, I hope so,' grannie said, 'in a year or two, when she knows her own mind a little better. I hear you have very gay doings at Stormouth Park; balls, and what not; private theatricals with lady actresses—a new fashion come in since my day; it must be very curious to see them.'

'Not at all curious, as they do things there; they've got all the best men from the officers' set at Plymouth, and a lady

cleverer than any common-place professional, Lady Di Hope Trevor, General
Hope Trevor's wife; a beautiful woman,
too.'

My curiosity was piqued; perhaps a
different feeling stirred, to hear him praise
another woman's beauty. ' Indeed!' I
cried; ' I would give anything in the world
to see them act.'

' You have never been to any of the
Stormouth theatricals?'

' No, never; but I should so like to!'

' Well, you shall, then; I'll ask Lady
Stormouth. I can promise you an invitation for Mrs. Fortescue and yourself. Next
Thursday evening you shall be there,' and
with this comfort he left me, bidding us
adieu.

CHAPTER III.

MY DEAREST FOE.

AND that was my first happy day! I
loved not without some return, and that
love was enough for me! I was more than
happy, I was satisfied. The hope to win
him, to be his wife, was far above my
humble passion; those who lived about
him, his intimates, the men under his command, his servants, might be blest as the
angels in heaven; his very dog I envied,
ay, even the inanimate things that formed
part of his daily life—as I might never do
—but he would cast into my bosom now
and again the sweet drops of comfort that
should make the taste of my young life
delicious for evermore!

To none but my own heart would I

confide the treasure of my secret joy, although that my grandmother indulged in was only second to it, and her hopes went far beyond mine in outspoken exultation at the prospect of so wonderful a conquest; she made sure that Arthur was struck with me, that he would follow it up, like a man of honour as he was, and that I should be married to him. 'Of course,' she added, by way of precaution, after bringing before my eyes a picture of such ecstasy as no sprinkling of cool caution could allay; 'of course, my child, you will not think of caring seriously for the man until he makes you an offer, as I have no doubt he will; but there's no way for a woman to lose a man like falling in love with him. I know you've been too sensibly brought up to be capable of such mawkish folly; but it makes me sick to see what fools girls are that way. You are very happy to have me to warn you; there is only one man in the world a woman should love—her husband. Now, there is such a person in the world, you know, as the man who is to be your husband, and you do him wrong in caring for anyone else; and until you are actually

married, you never can tell what may
happen, so you must not fall in love until
after you are married, and then you may
do so as much as ever you like.'

Very prudent, truly; only on these terms,
I should have preferred never to marry,
but to love only, without hope or aspiration
beyond love itself.

In due course arrived the promised
invitation from Lady Stormouth, but it
was not as we expected it, nor what my
grandmother quite liked; at first, indeed,
she refused to go on such terms. The list,
it stated, was full; every place would be
occupied in the room where the performance was arranged to take place; the
only seats remaining at Lady Stormouth's
disposal were in the gallery above at the
end of the room, and two of these were
placed at Mrs. Fortescue's choice. It was
a charity performance: guinea tickets to
the room; half guinea to the gallery.

'Well,' said grannie, taking her stand
upon her ruffled dignity, 'that's one way
of inviting people to your house, and a new
device for doing charity; I suppose Lady
Stormouth thinks I care to pay a guinea

for the honor of getting inside her doors;
and to the gallery, too! I have been received as an equal at the houses of earls
older in creation than her husband, whose
father got his title from that Whig king,
William IV.; the idea of making a first
and second class for your guests! I'll go
in the first, or not at all.'

'But it is merely a case of overcrowd-
ing,' I pleaded. 'I have set my heart so
on going! I would not miss it for all the
world. Do, grannie darling, let me have
my way for only this once, and I'll promise
never, never to ask anything you do not
wish again.'

'I was a beauty in my time,' urged the
old lady, 'a far greater beauty than any
you saw that night at the ball, or than you
will ever be—there's no vanity in saying
so now; it's all gone by; I was admired,
followed by men, hated and envied by
women, almost worshipped by the world;
and now, in my old age, to humor a little
chit, I'm to sit in the back kitchen to my
lady's parlour; oh no, oh no, at half
a guinea a seat!' and she burst into a
peal of scornful laughter. 'I'll write to

Lady Stormouth that I disdain the privilege.'

'Don't make an enemy of her, for my sake; consider, they are *his* intimate friends, both Lord and Lady Stormouth. Arthur is staying at their house; if you insult them, he can hardly visit us any more.'

'Well, there's something in that, certainly, but he ought to take our side; he ought to protect you from such a slight; it is an affront to himself.'

'Let us wait: he may not know. Why not send two guineas to Lady Stormouth and say, if she can give any extra seats, you will take them at that price, but not otherwise, for the benefit of the charity. Would not this be the most dignified way, not to see the affront at all, but show her we do not care about her?'

'Well, I don't approve of it; and I won't write it. Do you, if you like; but remember, unless Lady Stormouth sends tickets for the room, not the upper gallery, I don't go, nor you either.'

And so the matter was made up. I sent the two guineas and note on my grandmother's behalf, with our urgent request that such tickets might be sent as she could make use of, not in the gallery; but in any case her subscription should remain to the charity. Tickets for the room were sent in answer to this appeal.

We arrived early on the appointed evening, and passing into the great room, were duly saluted by Lady Stormouth, standing as hostess, in the vestibule, where every name was announced; beyond this no recognition was vouchsafed, except to private friends, and to these, we found, all the front rows of chairs were previously assigned; the general company of subscribers being handed into seats at the back. Arthur was nowhere to be seen when we came in. Later on, he entered by a side door with Lord Stormouth and other gentlemen staying at the house, and who rose from the dinner-table to attend the play.

This was the first amateur performance in a private mansion that I had ever witnessed, although not altogether inexperienced as a playgoer, having been several times to the theatre at Plymouth and Bristol; once, at the former, I had seen an officers' performance with regular actresses as the ladies. Now, I expected to see ladies act, and my impressions being yet new, I prefer to supplement them by the comments I overheard of a trio seated in front of us; they were a captain and his wife, rather a young couple, sharp and incisive, a thorough man and woman of the world, lately established in the neighbourhood, and admitted, like ourselves, as spectators; the third was a lady on a visit to the house, in middle life, with a kindly manner that attracted me. I took it into my head she was a literary celebrity from London. Of course, I caught none of their names.

The captain and his wife were first seated. On the lady afterwards joining them, he said, 'We came at eight o'clock, as we were bid, punctually; I see you know better; of course, we shall have to wait an unconscionable time.'

'I hope not; I heard everything was ready to begin.'

'Everything but the actors; amateurs never are, never can be up to time, except officers. We did it in style at the Plymouth theatre last time, but then we had regular actresses from London. I wish we were having them to-night.'

' My dear, you could not have actresses in a private house!' remonstrated his spouse.

' Then you shouldn't have acting in a private house, that's all ; amateur ladies think about nothing but their dress, and keeping people waiting two hours while they are enjoying themselves in their dressing-rooms ; and when they come on, they can't speak up to be heard ; it doesn't pay a fellow.'

' But the gentlemen have not left the dining-room,' put in the London lady.

'Oh, it's good fun for them, is it ? Awfully jolly, no doubt. I didn't dine here ; I had my dinner two hours earlier, and drove over, because Lady Stormouth sent me a circular, and my wife thought we ought to take tickets ; I can't see it at all.'

' My dear, we came to see the great hero, who is a guest in the house ; perhaps you can get introduced to him. And

Lady Diana Hope Trevor is to act. I
don't care how badly she does it : I would
not miss the sight on any account—not for
anything in the world.'

'She won't do it badly for an amateur ;
I hear she has been three months learning
the part, with Mrs. Cibber, a professional,
to coach her ; she repeats it all day long,
and keeps it up till two in the morning, till
the general puts out the lights and goes to
bed, because he won't have the servants
stop up so late as she does.'

'What a house he must have kept for
him, poor man !'

'You may say that, Nellie ; never you
take it into your head to act. If she were
my wife, I'd walk off and leave her spout-
ing—that's all.'

'Her husband is very proud of her acting,' interposed the London lady, 'and
most particular as to those she acts with,
and where she may appear.'

'She played at the Haymarket last season
for a benefit,' said the captain.

'Yes, the general gave his consent ; she
persuaded him, but he did not quite like
it. He is very proud of her talent.'

'Prouder of her altogether than he has good cause. I should see that plain enough if I were Sir John, and put a stop to her doings. Why, she's got herself invited here on purpose to throw herself in *his* way —you know whom I mean.'

'Hush, not a word about that here,' said the captain's lady. 'Look! the hero!'

A stir in the room and general commotion, as, the band playing the usual tune on such occasions, the hero of the night made his entrance, like a monarch in a play, with his attendant lords and gentlemen, and, with much ado on the part of everybody interested, was set in his appointed place, a high vantage ground, raised on steps, and canopied with Indian spoils and military trophies.

'Now they will begin, and I hope get it over in time to give us some supper before we set out on our long drive home,' reasoned the captain's lady; but an awful delay ensued—twenty minutes at least— before the prompter's loud whisper confided the signal 'ready' to the listening orchestra, an interval not unfilled by the captain's critical remarks.

'"The Green Bushes,"' he read out
from the pink satin programme. 'What a
notion! Madame Celeste's best part, the
only woman who ever could or should play
Miami.'

'Mrs. Cibber says Lady Diana is the
best who ever tried it, after Madame
Celeste, who is now too old to look the
part,' said the London lady.

'Mrs. Cibber says so, very likely, and so
she will say as long as my lady keeps her
purse strings open; if Di Hope Trevor
were a poor woman who wanted to make her
living on the stage, Mrs. Cibber wouldn't
teach her on credit for the sake of her
chance.'

At last, as all things mortal get done
with some time, the curtain went up for the
first act, which was suffered with decent
equanimity by the patient audience, all
expectation for the sight of Lady Diana,
who did not appear till the second act.
They were rewarded by a good deal of fun
at the expense of the performers, the stage
being crammed with what the captain called
'gentlemen supers, or superfine gentlemen,' made up as Irish peasants, whom all

the art of May and Clarkson could not transform from their proper selves; but sundry wonderful effects of the ludicrous were produced, which interfered in a most comical manner with the efforts of the principal characters. These last seemed to me quite as good as I had seen on the stage, but the captain (himself, I discovered, an amateur actor) would see no good thing in them.

Another long wait between the acts, filled in, however, with music, and ices handed round; then a preliminary scene of moderate dimensions at last ushered in the chief attraction. A shot was heard, and Lady Diana, in the habit of an Indian huntress, fowling-piece on shoulder, in shell-embroidered tunic and buskins, with mocassins bound on her feet, an *aigrette* surmounting her loose hair, and strange bead ornaments, stood before the assembly, a thing of beauty, whatever else she might be. I thought I had never seen so magnificent a piece of womanhood, out of canvas or marble: a tall and beautiful form, of which every outline was displayed, while decency could scarce complain that not

enough was hid. She was draped from
neck to knee; except the Juno-like arms,
bare to the shoulder, her face and throat
alone were uncovered; her colour only was
unlike the daughter of the wilds she
personated; a skin of milk, with the tint
upon her cheek such as the damask rose
changes to before it dies, or the cloud re-
flects as a memory of the sun's last kisses
when his face has gone down. No mortal
limner ever caught that heavenly hue! Her
grey eyes and dark-blonde tawny hair
were of true English breed, so were her
nose and upper lip, the perfection of aris-
tocratic race; rarest of all, her hands and
feet were but a little less small than my
own, which I inherited from my high caste
Indian mother, and had never yet seen
matched by a European.

How old was she? Involuntarily I
caught myself weighing that capital question as to the value of a woman's charms.
As I had once heard a lady say, beauty
was useless without youth, and youth without beauty. Surely she was much older
than I myself; twenty-eight, I should think,
perhaps thirty. Certainly she could not be

much more than that.　　I was fated, to en-
lightenment by the captain—'What a
splendid make up ! She looks quite a young
woman.'

His wife put up her opera-glass—
'Wonderful ! lots of white paint, of course ;
but that color's natural, and that hair is
all her own. Well, I call that wearing
splendidly, for a woman going on for fifty.'

'I don't believe she can be forty,' said
the London lady, taking a look through
the glass.

'My dear ! she was nearly forty when I
was a child.'

'A very fine woman of a little over
forty,' the captain settled it. 'Well, she
could wear anything, or nothing, and look
"fetching ;" and that's about what she can
do on the stage.'

'She is a born actress,' said the London
lady.

'Yes, but not a bred one ; can't move on
the stage—that's the test ; no idea of an
exit to music, can't play a part that depends
so much on pantomimic action. I grant
she speaks her words.'

'She is not like a trained actress, but a

woman in the same situation, with the same passion, would do the same things she does acting ; it may not be art, but it is true to nature.'

'Art is not mere nature, nor ever can be.'

'I know it ; but this woman carries away my feelings—I am moved, whether I approve or not.'

And so was I, and so were the most part of those five or six hundred spectators, too many to form a clique, and, therefore, more honest than critics or friends. The emotion crept through that cold, fashionable gathering, and stirred the very heart of the less sophisticated middle-class who packed the gallery. The quasi public, like a real public, were just, and the second act brought loud and long applause.

'And now,' said the captain, ' Lady Di is content to have the whole weight of the last act resting on her shoulders ; she has killed off the hero, at all events.'

'I can imagine a woman doing that in the situation,' said the London lady, taking the play *au serieux*. 'The Indian girl is deceived and betrayed ; he had a wife in

Ireland when he married her. Certainly
he deserves her revenge. It is very
natural in an Indian; an Englishwoman
could not shoot a man dead if she ever
loved him.'

' I don't know that ; shouldn't like to be
the happy man in Lady Di's case. She's
the woman to do it ; she played that scene
right well. Next act she has to repent,
and follow her lover to the grave ; she
won't be quite so good.'

She was, though. I felt the hot tears
roll down my cheeks, and grew sick and
faint, as she pourtrayed, too life-like, the
agonies of lingering death. Then my eyes
wandered in another direction, away from
the stage and its occupants, to Arthur,
where he sat. Ophelia like, I was watching the effect of the play on him. Most
wonderful! I saw his lofty brow bend
down, as it were, beneath the influence of
mighty magic ; the charm worked upon his
countenance ; eyebrow and lip were con-
tracted with strong pain, and struggled for
mastery with some emotion which the
proud man scorned to show. Here was a
revelation to me! A power was in that fair

woman to compel man's admiration by her
acting, inartistic as it was—a power that
grew upon one in that last scene, where
she had but to die, and this she did with
harrowing truth and reality. No want of
familiarity with the stage could mar her
effect in that, where she had but to sink in
her chair and slowly, miserably, yet bravely
die! It was too much for me to look upon
—no wonder it affected him to pain—but,
oh! how I envied her the power to touch
his heart so near.

Not that I suspected him of any wrong.
I knew she was married, and doubted not
that I was safe from an actual rival in her;
but the glory of her beauty and fame might
overpower the poor shadow in the dark
that crept around his feet in worship, not
daring to lift up eyes in hope upon one so
far above my sphere! Oh, how I envied
her!

Did my gaze attract that of others upon
him? So it seemed, for the spell of my
meditation was broken by a hushed laugh,
and the half whispered undertones of the
captain's lady. 'Look at him now! I
declare that's better than her acting! I

think he is caught in the toils. We shall
have some scenes enacted in a certain court
that will beat the excitement of this evening. Ah, Lady Di, you're very pretty, but
you're very naughty, I'm afraid!'

'Don't believe it ; the fellow is too clever
to be caught, or too lucky to be found out,'
said the captain. 'A man can draw out of
these things, if he knows how.'

'Oh, captain, speak for your own
experience, if you must, but don't throw
mud upon the greatest name in England :
'tis too unpatriotic—and besides—nobody
will believe you ; most certainly, if you
scandalise him, I shall never pay the least
attention to anything you say of anyone
again.'

So said the London lady, and put the
captain down. Happy she that could!
There was nothing left for me to do here,
but shrink into myself and hurry home.
I was not known, not wanted!

Disappointed and utterly disheartened,
I begged of my grandmother to come
away quickly. The crowd rose, and
pressed into the supper-room. At least, I
would not be thrust beneath his eye,

unfriended and neglected by his world, that
knew me not ; but we had not the choice,
being obliged to move with the throng, and
were drawn into the supper-room, where
a sumptuous spread did honor to the
hospitality of the house, and was accepted
as a boon by the audience, after their four
hours' sitting, even though, not being over
much 'given with welcome,' 'the feast was
sold ' in Lady Macbeth's sense.

My grandmother was faint, and wanted
wine. I struggled to the table, and tried
to obtain it for her. Oh, crown of humili_
ation! Arthur was looking at me! In a
moment I had shrunk into nothingness ; in
another, he had found me out, and stood
at my side ; he laid his hand upon my arm
so kindly—he helped me in my strait with
my grandmother, got us through to our
carriage, and handed us both in, but kept
my fingers in his clasp as he bade good-
night, with the wish of my heart granted in
a few words—' I shall see you soon,' and
then he hurried back to the splendid scene ;
but I knew that she was nothing to him,
and that I—oh, Paradise on earth! what
might not be ?

CHAPTER IV.

AGAINST THE WORLD.

HE kept his word, and quickly too. Twice was I blest : that he came to me, and that he came so soon ! Came he in love, or in friendship, or in merest courtesy, I cared not ; was it not enough to look upon him ? to hear him speak to me ? But I was made to feel by my grandmother that she received him as my suitor, or had no welcome for him. He was not to play the angel on her Berlin broidered hearth-rug with impunity for me !

She had more reason than I, or it looked very like it, though Arthur proved fully at his ease, master of himself and the situation, whether he turned his conversation to my grandmother or to me. He spoke seriously, as seeking information, but in the kindest way, as to our present position and family surroundings, questions such as a man of the world, however much in love, likes to have satisfactorily answered, and failing this, often makes a merit to himself of ' not being so far gone for a woman as not to listen to reason.' Who we were, and what we came from was all right. My present place in the world, at least, was all wrong, but so as to be remedied at once, by an honorable man, whose love was true.

' I can understand Lady Stormouth not going out of her way to find you out,' said Arthur, on my grandmother's declaration that she would never care for the honor of entering Stormouth Park again ; ' she has two sons whom she wants to see married to two earls' daughters, of three hundred years' creation at least, Stormouth being rather a new title. Not but what a Fortescue is better than many an earl, in my opinion.'

' Better in our own, I hope, than to lay traps for her ladyship's two fools of sons. I am sure they are safe from us ; what do you say to that, Lily ?'

'I say she takes me for what I am not,' said I, reddening; 'but she has plenty to do if she means to protect her sons from half the girls in the county, who occupy themselves in tuft hunting because they have nothing else to do; she may trust me —I hate a crowd.'

'I saw the Honorable Hubert making eyes at you, but he could find no one to introduce him,' said Arthur, maliciously.

'Perhaps so, because I did not want him; I believe that's the way with men.'

'Ay, you've found that out already, Miss Leila; that's the way with women, we may retort; you find the pleasure is as great of being hunted as to hunt. You've heard of Galatea, who threw out the bait in shape of an apple, and ran away, knowing her lover was sure to follow and catch her in her hiding-place.'

'The Honorable Hubert will not follow me; I'm not in his set, grannie says.'

'You ought to be; but women are so unkind to each other; they find you too charming, too attractive; if you were an ordinary girl, you would be among the first people in the county. Lady Augusta St. Aubyn is your cousin, I believe ?'

'Distantly connected,' said grandmother stiffly. 'A younger son of our family married the heiress of the title, early in this century, and our estate followed the male line. My son having no child but Leila, they have the inheritance. But it does not seem to have done much good with them.'

'I see, then, why there is a coldness. I was speaking of you to Lady Augusta yesterday, Leila, asking whether she knew how exquisitely you sang, and would you guess her answer ? "There are too many women who sing," she said, and so I would not propose to introduce you.'

'Quite right,' said grannie.

'Tell her I said there are too many women old maids,' I put in, wickedly.

'Oh, you bitter creature! there you have poor Lady Augusta at your mercy. She's safe to be Lady Augusta St. Aubyn to the day of her death, and as proud of her title and position as if she were seventeen. Well, they're not worth your voice, Leila, and less gifted people should beware how they tread on your dainty little toes, that I see. But you have not told me how you enjoyed Lady Diana Hope Trevor's performance. What did you think of it?'

'I think her the most beautiful woman I ever saw.'

'I am glad to hear you say that.'

'Why? It is simply true.'

'Well, perhaps that is why; but there are a great many reasons more than I could undertake to analyse. But I am pleased to hear a girl like you say so. I have always thought her beautiful.'

'You have known her very long?'

'Oh! years and years, in India. There was not a girl came out there from England in all my time that would be looked at beside her. She drove half the men mad. A fellow would gallop hundreds of miles to a ball on the chance of getting a dance with her. But there never was, never will be, such another beauty under the sun.'

I was growing jealous. What could she be to him? I repeated his words—'never was, never will be, such another beauty under the sun.' 'You think so, *you*—' I

faltered. Arthur laughed away my blame
with—

'Oh, she's *passée* now—three-and-forty.
I did not mean to put her in comparison
with young girls. In her own imperial
way she is superb.'

'She looked wonderfully young that
night, and acted wonderfully.'

'She is an enthusiast in acting, and
enthusiasm carries an audience or a breach
as nothing else can. You are an enthusiast,
my young Saint Cecilia—you did not see
the faults.'

'Yes, I did, plenty of them ; you forget,
I am a trained singer, which helps me to
judge an artist in another line. Lady
Diana has a good speaking voice, but she
lets it fall when she should keep it up,
drops half her sentences, so that she could
not be heard where we sat ; catches her
breath with a gasp, as a singer is taught
not to do ; and then, the passages in a
speech are like the phrases of music, you
must know how to manage the changes
from one to another ; she does not. She
will give one part very well, and another
part very well, with something between
the two that spoils the effect.'

'I know what you mean ; she fails in the transitions from one emotion to another; the most difficult thing in acting. Well, that's her weakest point, except tripping on her train, which sometimes happens to her when she gets excited.'

'I never thought of that. She carried me out of myself; take her altogether, I never saw such acting before.'

'You have not seen much. I can tell you, they ran after her playing in India, where we see no acting at all, except amateurs'; all the officers who can act catch the infection. I used to be fond of it myself, at one time.'

'Did you ever act with her ?'

'Sometimes—very long ago. I had to give it up, when I had too much upon my hands. Have you ever tried acting ?'

'Not yet. I would give anything in the world I could, if you—I should like to act with you, I think I could,' said I, restraining myself.

'Why should we not, if you like it ? I will organise a performance with the officers ; they did beg of me to join them, but I declined. I will accept now, for your sake.

What shall we play ? Do you like Desdemona ?'

'Just what I should have chosen ; but
how can I do it ? I have never stood
upon a stage, and everyone will know
me.'

'Acting is not fit for young girls,' interposed grannie ; 'you must wait till you are
married, Lily, and then it must depend
upon your husband. I cannot give my
consent to such a thing, except in a private
room ; you cannot act in public with the
officers.'

'It shall be a private performance,' said
Arthur ; 'we'll take the Assembly Room
here. You don't boast of a theatre in Stormouth, and that's perhaps all the better.
We'll entertain the county better than a
ball.'

That was settled ; grannie, looking at it
in the light of a positive advance on
Arthur's part, withdrew her opposition to
what she did not quite approve.

'But I shall not know how to act. How
can I ?' I pleaded, nervously, wishing to
be overborne.

'I will teach you,' said Arthur, gently.

'Othello was once a favourite part of mine, when I could get the chance to play it. A great undertaking for amateurs, but we have done it, and well too. We have several good men here now, and I have got the time, for a wonder. I'm stationary at Stormouth Park for six weeks to come.'

'You will teach me yourself?'

'I'll ride over three or four times a week, and rehearse with you. Learn your words first.'

'I have read the play so often, I shall soon learn Desdemona; but what lady will be able to take Emilia? Is not that a difficult part?'

'Very, but we'll find a way through the difficulty; I'll bring down Mrs. Heathcote from town, and her husband shall be our stage-manager; they often play with the officers.'

'An actress!' exclaimed grannie; 'you don't intend Leila to associate with an actress?'

'She is a most proper woman, several ladies visit her; and 'tis only what amateurs always come to—a little professional help

sometimes. I don't know an amateur lady
who could play Emilia without making the
whole thing ridiculous, except Lady Di, if
she chose.'

'And why can't Lady Di play it, if you
ask her?' inquired grannie.

'I won't have Lady Di,' said Arthur,
determinately, and carried his point, as he
was bound to do; there was a touch of
bitterness in his decision which, to my mind,
jarred somewhat harshly with his former
praise of the beautiful *dilettante*. I ques-
tioned him.

'Did Lady Di ever play Desdemona
with you?'

'Well, yes, she did on one occasion.'

'And she would not play Emilia now,
with me as Desdemona?'

'I should not care to have her, that's just
about it. It is best that no other star
should twinkle too close to her sphere.
Have you seen the article in the *Empress*?'

'No. What was that?'

'I'll send you a copy, or bring you one
the day after to-morrow. We'll read Desdemona through together.'

With this he bade adieu, and during his absence, prolonged to four days instead of two, arrived the newspaper. The article ran thus :

'On Wednesday, 24th, a splendid entertainment took place at Stormouth Park, Cornwall, the ancestral seat of the noble Earl and Countess, the charitable object of assisting the funds of the Stormouth Hospital furnishing occasion for the most delightful treat ever witnessed in the county, the acting of Miami in the " Green Bushes" by the most beautiful and accomplished amateur actress in all England, the Lady Diana Hope Trevor. It would be invidious to draw comparisons with any actress on the stage as an exponent of the part ; but it is well known in critical circles that Lady Diana ensures perfection in every character she undertakes, by an amount of assiduity unequalled by any other artist, on or off the stage, and her personation, while elaborately true to nature, gave evidence in every sentence, as in every action, of the careful training of the first of professional instructresses. Further to describe details would be in bad taste ; we will therefore

restrain our pen, only assuring our fair
leaders of fashion that they may well be
proud before the distinguished world of
artists and men of letters of the triumph
achieved by their queen, unparalleled
hitherto by any amateur actress, whether
we look at her own surpassing charms, or
the delight of all those favored by the
high privilege of being admitted among the
brilliant assembly where shone out, conspicuous by his own fame, as well as by his
visible appreciation of the artistic banquet
displayed, the illustrious presence of ——,'
here an enumeration of Arthur's qualities
and titles, in which the pen of the writer
ran raving mad, the name of the lady's husband being brought in incidentally, quite
at the end of the rhapsody, by way of
propriety in the conclusion drawn, I
suppose, by the judicious critic.

Certainly this came as a token of remem-
brance, yet I should have been almost
better pleased had Arthur left me to think
my own thoughts undisturbed, until we met
again. Against all this prestige, how
should I stand the test of comparison in his
eyes, unless—unless their looks were other

than the world's ? I must try it by the proof.

Oh, vanity of vanities of men ! But why did he send it to me, to read such praises of him as that ? He did not need them.

CHAPTER V.

HOPE DEFERRED.

WHETHER Arthur undertook his task for mere love of acting, for the pleasure of giving me pleasure, or for pure love of me, is a problem I shall never solve; I know that, as he taught me to play at making love, he grew to me day after day; we were Othello and Desdemona in terrible earnest.

'I loved him for the dangers he had passed, and he loved me that I did pity them.'

Of course I had to learn every movement of the stage 'business,' as it is called ; grannie letting matters take their own course, because she looked upon our love making as no stage playing, but the frank

familiarity of an engaged couple with each
other ; once or twice she interrupted us,
and told Arthur he must not shock his
audience by carrying acting too far. 'We
are supposed to be married,' was Arthur's
excuse, and she took it as if it were a fact,
and, as my future husband, let him have
his way ; it would have needed much
prudery to be offended with that, so tender,
so delicately gentle, was the fond caress
that added eloquence to his words.

I was to sing in the last scene, where
Shakespeare gives a swan-like song of fare-
well to the young wife appointed to death.
What had I to do with her—I, who was
past all expressing happy in my new-born
love ? my expectation, Eden on earth with
him ! Yet a sweet sad melody came to me,
to sing in low recitative, wild and mournful
as despair could chant. It was beautiful,
he said, and would draw tears from a stone,
and we wept together ; but these were
tears of exceeding joy ! Without words we
understood each other.

Shortly before the performance, we had
general rehearsals at the Assembly Rooms,
Mr. and Mrs. Heathcote presiding ; she

had a good deal to do with me, as Emilia, and took me in hand, in her experienced professional way, to advise me on various matters ; my dressing and making up—of the latter I of course knew nothing—were her especial charge ; also my general carriage of myself through my forthcoming ordeal ; Othello had no right to kiss me, she said, being played by an amateur ; adding : ' I am sure he will not do it ; he knows better than to draw remarks in front, as you are not on the stage ; with us, it is of no consequence, in the regular way of business ; an actor does not want to kiss you, especially when he sees you take no notice of him, which is the best way ; I have never known them to do anything out of impertinence beyond mere ' stage kissing ;' but with private gentlemen, 'tis another matter ; they will do it in earnest, if they have the chance. I should not like to hear any of them boast he had kissed Miss Fortescue ; you'll have to take care of yourself if you act often. I wish you had a mother to look after you ; I would not be responsible for the charge of you on any consideration in the world. I think you would be very apt to get into mischief.'

' I shall be equal to the situation, never fear, and obliged to you for putting me on my guard for another time; but I am safe with my Othello now—I know him.'

' You think you know him, bless the child ! Then you know nothing about it. You ask him who gave him that ring on his little finger, that he never takes off. Next time you have an opportunity, ask him that.'

' What, that beautiful diamond ring ? A present from some great person, no doubt; some Indian prince, perhaps : he has had many presents.'

' Nonsense ! 'tis an English made ring ; don't you know the difference from an Indian one ?'—I had forgotten that—'a ring to fit a lady's finger, but not so tiny as yours. What little fingers you have, and, oh, what nails, thin as tissue paper ! No wonder you have them break,' and she burst out laughing at my hand, as it lay under examination in the middle of one of her broad palms. She had given me something to think about

The next opportunity I had with Arthur alone, I put forth all my cunning to ascertain what I was ashamed to question him upon, the history of that ring I had often admired, but now could have torn off his little finger, and, like Harry Hotspur's wife, broken his little finger too. My device was to draw his attention to a ring I wore on my wedding finger; it had been my mother's, an Indian ruby set with pearls. As he held my hand looking at it, I bade him take it off and try it on his own. He obeyed, and it stuck at the first joint.

'It's too small for you,' I said.

'Rather.'

I laughed at my own little trick, and fixing my eyes on the obnoxious diamond beneath—

'Try yours on me,' I said. 'On my third finger, I think it would just fall off.'

'Not there—that's the engaged finger; it would be unlucky. Not that ring.'

'Try it on any finger you like, then. I want to see the diamond.'

'What a child! can't you see it on my hand?'

'I don't like to see it on your hand. I hate to see it—why won't you take it off?'

His brow darkened.

'Some one has been talking to you about that ring, Leila. Who was it?'

'I'll tell you if you'll take it off.'

'Well, I will then. There, 'tis off now. Who spoke to you about it?'

'Mrs. Heathcote told me some lady gave it you.'

'The woman's a fool to speak to you of such a thing. She knows nothing about it.'

'But it *was* a lady gave it you?'

'As you ask me, Leila, it was. I will not tell you anything but the truth. It would be no use, for you would not believe me.'

'A lady gave it you, and you will not allow me to put it on. I hope there was nothing wrong in her giving it to you.'

'Nothing but what was honorable.'

'Then why must not I put it on?'

'Because I promised that no one should except myself.'

'That was a strange promise. Are you engaged to the lady?'

'Leila, how can you think such a thing of me? Certainly not.'

'Perhaps she is a married woman.'

'What put that into your head?'

'Do you flirt with married women? They say men are fond of flirting with married women.'

'Married women are fond of flirting with men sometimes.'

'Do you make love to them?'

'You should blame your own sex if we do, Leila; no man, sitting at another man's table, would dare to make an advance to his friend's wife, unless he saw the way open to draw him on; it is the woman who tempts us astray.'

'But you—you would not let yourself be tempted?'

'I am not better than others.'

'I think you are, much better, as I know you are much greater than any other man.'

'Don't you know, Leila, if a beautiful woman loves a man, the best of us is in her power?"

'No, no; you are too honorable for that. I never thought of your doing anything wrong, or capable of it; if I had I could not trust you as I do.'

'Trust me for ever and ever, you, Leila, in the innocence of your heart; you understand nothing of these things—it would be a profanation to attempt to explain them to you. A pure, unmarried girl can attract no affection but what is honorable; it is different with a married woman; she knows what she is doing, but in this case of the ring, there was no harm; I pledge you my honor.'

'Then can you tell me whose it was?'

'I cannot.'

'And why? if I do not offend you by asking.'

'Well, Leila, if you must know, it was or seemed to be a love-affair on her part. I thought so, and that if she so wished, it was not the man's place to hold back; not that I really cared for her, but we had been fond of one another when we were young. However, she was good, and I was very glad that she repulsed me.'

'But she gave you her ring. Why?'

'She would wish me to marry her if her husband died.'

'Oh, Arthur!'

'But I would never do that. I could not like her enough to marry her.'

'She believes that you would.'

'If she does I cannot help it.'

'And if her husband dies?'

'That's very unlikely; he is a strong man for his age; a better life than I am.'

'But if he should die, what would you do?'

'Keep out of her way. I would not have her for my wife, after going so far as she ought not to have done.'

'Your wife must be like Cæsar's, without suspicion.'

'Just so, Leila, pure as virgin snow.'

'Oh, men, men!'

'Oh, women, women! we might say. Beware of your own sex, Leila. No man will ever intend you harm; but do you know that when a woman is thoroughly bad, she is ten thousand times worse than any man?'

'It may be so. This one that gave you the ring—did you make her any promise? Have you bound yourself to marry no one else—to wait for her husband's death?'

'Leila, how could you imagine—a
woman that could do such a thing—have I
not told you I would never marry her?'

'But you have not told me you were not
bound to remain as you are—free.'

'I am not, I could not be bound to any
such thing under the circumstances ; why,
she never was anything to me."

'She was in love with you ; that is
everything to a woman.'

'You know nothing about such things,
Leila ; you talk like a child.'

'I am no child; I can feel like a
woman. If my heart were broken, I could
die.'

'God forbid, my dear child; I am not
worthy of such an affection.'

'I did not mean—I hope I have not said
what I ought not ;' I sobbed out pitifully.

'You have said nothing, done nothing
but what I honor you for, my poor innocent
child ; it is I who am to blame.'

'Then you do not—care for me—at
all.'

'I love you, darling ; you are the first
woman I have truly loved in all my life ;
but you are too young, too guileless, too

angel like. It is I who am not worthy of you.'

'How can you say that? you, the greatest hero in the world! it would be a heaven on earth to die for you.'

'My darling! will you live for me then? will you take me as I am, with all my faults, and never reproach me for the past that cannot be recalled? All we have to do, is to make the best of the time to come.'

'I will live and die for a few kind words of yours; I am your own to do what you will with me.'

'She trusts me without a doubt or fear! One day you shall know everything concerning me.'

'And her—you will tell me her name?'

'No, never, Leila; that is not my own secret. You should not ask me to tell you that; it would not be honorable.'

'I did not think of it that way. Forgive me. Then that one secret must remain between us for ever?'

'It must.'

Had I not eyes? Should I ever see him and Diana Hope Trevor together, if it was

she, I should need no tongue to tell me
so; if it was not she, most probably I
should never know who it was, and should
trouble myself the less, that it was not she;
but that some woman had had him at her
feet was not without stings of jealousy for
me.

He pressed my hands most tenderly, and
kissed them, that was all. He did not
clasp me to his heart as he might have
done, but he looked at me; that look was
enough. I was deeply blest beyond my
heart's desire, though I knew not, scarce
asked myself, whether we were engaged
or not.

CHAPTER VI.

MAKETH THE HEART SICK.

I LOOKED forward to the consummation of my happiness, in our playing together as Othello and Desdemona. My part so entirely in tune with the emotions of my heart, his giving him excuse for the fond caresses so delicately forborne, and which I knew, under pretext of acting, he would steal upon me. An intrigue at the last moment all but defeated my hopes; of my envied conquest I was not yet secure!

As I have already hinted, I was allowed to act upon condition that the performance should be a private one. Cards of invitation were printed in Arthur's name, and duly sent to the local aristocracy; a gallery being set apart for dependants and humble

friends, with admission by another form of
ticket.   Need I say the anxiety to be
invited of those who had not quite a claim
to the distinction was something quite
beyond the ordinary eagerness of country
folk to obtain tickets for any exclusive
county ball, or other entertainment, to
which money could help them, on charitable
grounds ? A means was found to supply
the demand in the present case, by somebody (never discovered) purloining a couple
of dozen invitation cards out of a private
drawer of Arthur's.   These were sold at a
guinea a piece, at a library in the town, connected with the Assembly Rooms, and were
all eagerly bought up before the trick was
discovered by the sellers, who declared
they received them through the post, in
Arthur's own name, with instructions to
dispose of them for the benefit of the
County Hospital, to which institution the
money had been duly paid in.   Arthur
was exceedingly annoyed, but said it would
be invidious now to disturb the matter, the
parties having evidently acted in good
faith, in consequence of a hoax performed
by some mischief-maker in the back-

ground, who would only be gratified by any scandal arising.

My old enemy, Mrs. Grundy, took the case up, and attacked my grandmother on my account, the result being, I was forbidden to attend rehearsal the next day, grannie declaring the talk of the people would kill her if I did not give up the performance. I was in agonies, and actually went down on my knees to beg that she would relent, but in vain. I could not outrage her feelings, however inconsistent and unreasoning, so I sent a note to Arthur, by the maid who usually attended me to rehearsal at the Assembly Rooms, and informed him I had a difficulty with my grandmother on account of the sale of tickets; that I hoped to get over it in a day or two, and begged him, for this once, to let Mrs. Heathcote read my part for me.

After a day passed by me in misery, dreading that all would be upset by my enforced absence, Mrs. Heathcote, in vehement agitation, rushed into the house late in the afternoon.

' Do you mean to throw up your part?'

she exclaimed. 'Was that the meaning of
your note? I say it was not. I read for
you, my dear; I allowed no one else to do
it. Lady Di was there with her husband,
to be sure, on pretence of asking for
another card for friends. I saw through
her at once.'

'What did she do?' I gasped, breath-
less.

'Said Desdemona was her favourite part,
she could play it at an hour's notice. You
know this is the last rehearsal but one; we
play the day after to-morrow; she had the
dress ready, she said. She knew a girl
like you, who had never appeared before,
was sure to break down at the last. She
would show, if she were allowed, she said
to Arthur, what a great part Desdemona
was for one who could feel it. She would
prove what a depth of feeling and passion,
and so on, all the time we were rehearsing.'

'And did Arthur give way to her?'

'What could the poor man do? He had
to show your note to account for your
absence; he was very nervous himself about
you. Lady Diana told him Mrs. Fortescue

would never allow you to play, and gave
her great credit for her decision.'

'Oh, Grannie, after giving me leave at
first! I must play. Do you want to have
me die? It would be better for me than to
be put down by such a trick.'

'A trick, my dear, you've said it,' blurted
out Mrs. Heathcote. 'Those cards were
stolen and sold on purpose to keep you
out of your chance. I mention no names,
mind; it's all very clever, but they can't
hoodwink me. I know every plank on the
boards, amateur as well as professional,
bless you!'

Grandmother wavered, halting between
two opinions. Mrs. Heathcote plunged
in to the rescue.

'Do you want to see that child snuffed
out like a tallow candle by a woman with
a handle to her name? Let her act;
gracious goodness! what's the hubbub
about a few tickets being sold for a charity?
If it were the whole roomful it would be all
the better for her. Nothing like a paying
audience; save me from friends and paper!
Let her act, in heaven's name, or the child
will break her heart.'

And so grannie yielded. Next day we rehearsed in peace, but it was bitter to me to think another, not Arthur, had taken my part in my need.

The night came, and a splendid audience packed the room from foot-lights to ceiling. Music began, and I knew that within a quarter of an hour I must face the ordeal which, the first time, has so much of the nature of hot ploughshares to the young aspirant's feet.

At the side between the wings I met Arthur, beaming with approval at my bridal attire.

'Desdemona,' he whispered, and took my hand. It trembled fearfully; I was still suffering from the recent agitation I had been put through. 'You are nervous?' he inquired—the way to make me so.

'Not so much so that I cannot conquer it, I trust,' was my answer, in low tones.

He took another alarm: 'Your voice—it is not gone?'

'No, I am saving it for my trial'—I spoke half raising it, to show him there was nothing to fear—'trust me, I will do my best—better than you have seen me yet—you shall be proud of me.'

Success, darling!' he whispered, and we parted as the curtain rose. He was to come on the opposite side to me, and there was scarce room, after the play began, to cross the small make-shift stage.

I stood watching him, while he appeared, the hero of the hour, before the expectant audience. I drank in the cheers that hailed him, prolonged for several minutes, before he could speak a word, all my mind and spirit, together with my eyes, were drawn out towards him, until I lost all thought for myself ; then something made me give a great start : it was Mrs. Heath-cote laying her arm on my shoulder, and whispering in my ear : ' Don't mind him, my dear, fancy he's only a stuffed man : mind nobody but yourself, and you'll do ; if you please the public, you'll please him well enough, so don't you get excited, mind.'

I took the warning, and strove to put away my very love from my heart. How strange it all was ! so unlike the delight I had anticipated. All sensation seemed to leave me as I came on for my first scene. How I got through it I have no recollection; all I knew was, there rose a warm sound of welcome for me, and a murmur of praise after I spoke my words, and, in my half consciousness, I was aware of him near me. Then I became dimly sensible that I was doing a hard thing; coming short of my own intentions; I caught myself falling into the very same faults I had censured in Lady Diana. Thus I knew myself an inexperienced actress, but I got through.

'You are more nervous than you thought you would be,' said Arthur, kindly, as he took me off with him. 'Courage, dearest, and you must have a great success.'

'Speak up louder this next act—louder,' said Mrs. Heathcote, as she came on with me for the scene at Cyprus. The steady, reliable actress was a great support to me while we were on the stage together. Arthur excepted, I never felt so safe with the rest; each seemed rather to act independently for himself than to play to the others, although they were all clever, and well drilled for amateurs.

I had made the plunge, and the worst was over; the enthusiasm of the audience floated us on with the rising tide; Othello

and Desdemona meet; the sweet words
melt like honey into my heart :

'If it were now to die
'Twere now to be most happy, for I fear
My soul hath her content so absolute
That not another comfort like to this
Succeeds in unknown fate.'

Then came the kiss, his first kiss, upon
my brow, another on my cheek; it was
enough; I felt then I could die even thus,
and ask no . more of joy beneath the sun.
It was fortunate I had not to speak
afterwards during that scene ; my power to
do so was quite gone.

The third act rose upon the audience
with the grandeur of a storm, sweeping
them off their feet, as I heard one say.
Mrs. Heathcote, with her critical acumen,
remarked that Arthur's was the 'most
powerful, but most unequal performance of
Othello,' she had ever played to.

In the fourth act a most effective incident—not usually presented on the stage
—was restored, where Shakespeare makes
Othello fall into a trance, fainting under
Iago's torturing stabs of jealousy ; and on
his recovery the 'demi-devil' sets him to

7—2

listen while Cassio, speaking of another
woman, Bianca, appears by contrivance to
give conclusive testimony of Desdemona's
sin, finally, Bianca, entering, produces the
fatal handkerchief, and Othello, convinced
by eye and ear, rushes on to madness, and
murder of the thing he loves.   Another
restoration was in the opening of the fifth
act, where instead of lying on my bed
before the curtain rose, I appeared with
Emilia unbinding my hair, and sang my
song as I prepared for sleep, the only opportunity I had for display of my best
talent—the gift of voice.   Here I knew
beforehand I should achieve a triumph, and
I did it.   With dying notes I glided into
my curtained alcove, and Othello entered
the chamber.   Then every breath was
hushed, and he went on with the awful
scene.

It was over ; I was standing before the
footlights by Arthur's side, bending before
the crowd I dared not look upon, tasting of
the sweet breath of applause I had earned
so well—they told me I had, both Mrs.
Heathcote and Arthur, that my success,
with all drawbacks, was complete and un-

questionable.   I would not cross the stage :
I shrank back out of sight, and left Arthur
to receive his honors alone : my eyes were
fixed upon him, and yet I perceived in an
opposite corner, where a kind of private
box had been erected, and from whence
only I could be seen, Lady Diana,
seated, with her eyes fixed upon me like
two gleaming daggers ; such a look of hate
and revenge I had never conceived in
imagination before. Was it my own success
she envied, or the share I took in Arthur's ?
That was the question I wanted answered
now !

CHAPTER VII.

TRUST ME ALL IN ALL.

THAT question I still felt reluctant to press upon Arthur, fearing to displease him. Some days later it arose of itself in an unexpected form.

As we were at breakfast one morning, Grannie and I, a newspaper came in by post addressed to me. It was the last number of the *Empress*, the same periodical which gave Lady Diana such fulsome adulation on her performance at Stormouth Park. Surely this number contained some notice of Othello on Arthur's account, perhaps some flattering encouragement to me as Desdemona! Exulting in the thought, I exclaimed to Grannie when I found the article. Woe worth the day, as I read on!

Thus ran the critique: 'On Tuesday last an amateur performance of Othello was given at Stormouth Assembly Rooms, Cornwall, under the auspices of our great national hero, who himself delighted the local magnates and *beau monde* of the county by his magnificent impersonation of the noble Moor, a character so much in harmony with his own. A picked company of distinguished amateurs from the corps of officers stationed at Plymouth ably supported him; valuable professional aid being rendered by Mrs. Heathcote as Emilia, so that (with one important exception) there was a completeness as well as talent displayed such as is seldom to be met in a performance arranged for one night only. The principal exception, to which we must allude, was in the part of Desdemona, played in a manner so inefficient as sadly to detract from the interest in every scene where the heroine appeared, and seriously to hamper the efforts of the gallant officer in the opposite part. The *young* lady— this was her only excuse—whose name we forbear to mention, being one at least associated with that of a noble family in Devon,

with which, we were informed, she is in no
way connected—the lady in herself pos-
sesses no one qualification of any kind for
the part she assumed, unless we may
except a strong singing voice, such as we
have heard from itinerant ballad singers,
wholly without cultivation or control, but
which served as a pretext to drag in the
" Willow Song " by Desdemona in her night-
dress, long expunged by good taste from
the acting edition of Othello.   It would be
hard to play Desdemona worse, or look it
worse, and we should hope the good sense
and   taste   of   the   lady's   friends   would
obviate, for her own sake, any repetition of
the display.'

I did not drop the paper; I clutched it
fast.   Nothing was left now but to conceal
it from Grannie, if I could, having im-
prudently roused her curiosity.   But she
was too sharp to be hoodwinked by any
poor stratagem of mine.   As I was trying
to tear the paper to pieces, she caught it
out of my hand with a strong grasp, and
read it all, uttering aloud, word by word,
the worst passages as she read, with a
cruelty of deliberation to thrust the knife

home, and turn it round and round in the
gash, both to herself and me.

'Now, Lily, that's the consequence of
not taking advice from me. I told you, I
begged of you, I knew you would be utterly
and irretrievably ruined ; no girl could ever
get over such a thing. But you would not
take my advice.'

Here was a grain of truth to make my
bread of humiliation bitter ! From a child
she had gently suffered me to 'gang my
ain gait' in most things ; then, at the most
critical point of my life, she had spasmodi-
cally striven to rein me in, and failing to do
so, if any ill came of it, on my shoulders
her blame would light; worst of all, even
in her eyes, which had seen nothing but
what was to be praised in my first attempt,
enough of the mud thrown by the critic
seemed to stick upon me to turn my very
merits into newly discovered faults. What
could I expect from the rest of the world ?

'To disgrace your family, your poor
father's memory !' she pursued.

'No,' I cried out; 'this is done on
purpose ; a trick and a slander. I will
have it answered ; I shall appeal to Arthur ;

I know he will do me right. This is an insult to him through me.'

' Let him take it so, and protect you ; or do you have done with him ; my son's daughter must throw herself under no man's feet to be made little of in this way; he must right you, or you shall have done with him.'

' I doubt not he will,' I said, assuming confidence, though my heart misgave me as to his standing up for me against Lady Diana ; my whole anxiety was bent to conceal that cause of suspicion at least from grandmother.

' He must be explicit—there must be an engagement between you, understood and acknowledged, or you must give him up ; we are not to be made fools of. I will speak to him plainly.'

' No I forbid it ; I implore you to do nothing, Grannie ; I had rather never see him again than be put to such shame ! Leave it to me, for the mercy of God !'

' Do as you will, then ; I wash my hands of the business ; remember, I am warning you in time ; you will have to give up that man, after the disgrace he has brought upon you.'

It was too true. What had I to do
with thrusting myself before the world in
the fierce light of his fame? To be
humbled for the rest of my life, like a poor
burnt fly, dragged half dead out of the
hot wax of a candle! A modern Semele
to a Jove with an unacknowledged but
malignant Juno to corrupt him to my
detriment; another Ino to be stung by all
the gadflies bred of Mrs. Grundy's tongue!
I could not, I would not bear it; I would
appeal to Arthur, who alone could lift me
out of my trouble! Surely he would not
let my life be made hateful to me?

I did so when he came, but he met me
coldly, and merely said it was best to take
no notice, it was not worth while; they
had no right to criticise a private performance at all, and it was most impertinent;
but, no names being mentioned, it was
best to treat it with silent contempt. I
had not much patience, I was vexed past
what little I had.

'Arthur,' I said, 'is it not every word
of it utterly false?'

'I think so,' he said, smiling. 'Is not
that enough for you? Never mind any-

one; you are charming; they would not
have hit you so hard, only they thought
you too strong to be easily put down; the
Empress is written by women; so what
would you have?'

'Arthur, do you know what I believe?
—shall believe all my life, unless you
prove to me the contrary—Lady Diana
got me this attack through jealousy—not
mere jealousy of my acting, I mean, but of
my playing with you. I believe she is
jealous—because of you. Is this true?'

'I do not think it likely.'

'You deny it faintly. I do believe it is
true; I know she wanted to thrust me out of
my part, and you—you nearly let her do it.'

'Leila, you will make me really angry,
and I certainly shall not answer any such
questions; any lady who shows me the
slightest favor is safe as to my respecting
her confidence. As a man of honor, what
else could I do? Put yourself in the
situation.'

'I could not be in the situation. She
is married.'

'No, you could not; but supposing such
a case with any woman; say she had com-

mitted herself ever so little, or ever so much, what must the man be to betray her ? A man with any feeling would give up his life, before he would speak a word to injure her.'

'Then I am not in your confidence ; this suspicion must remain for ever like a barrier between us ?'

'Leila, beware of suspicion, if you love.'

'Arthur, I believe that Lady Diana loves you.'

'You have no right to think so ; you will give both yourself and me a great and useless pain by imagining such a thing.'

'Will you give me your word of honor there is no cause to think so ?'

'If you like, Leila ; but under any circumstances I should feel bound to do that to shield any woman from the unjust suppositions of another. Do not give way to a censorious temper, Leila ; I never expected it from you.'

'You did not, and you say to me that to screen a bad woman you would tell a lie.'

'Well, I will put it to yourself: suppose a man were put upon his word of honor to tell the truth; should he do so, if it involved disgrace and ruin to a woman, but to himself—well, much less than to her—should he tell the truth and betray her?'

'No, but he could be silent.'

'But if silence involved confession, would it not in that case be a less crime to deny the charge?'

'Well, perhaps it might be; I am a bad judge; I do not understand this code of honor—or dishonor; women ought not to do these things.'

'They ought not; but I will put it to an extreme case: if a man were upon his oath in court, is he not bound rather to perjure himself than tell of a woman?'

'No; no man can ever be bound to call the name of God to witness a lie—not for any woman should a man give up his soul.'

'Even this he should do rather than give up a woman; that is the act of a coward.'

'Then if a man should swear falsely to

screen a guilty woman, how could an innocent one falsely accused be cleared by a man's oath? You would have no possible redress for calumny.'

'I did not think of that. I believe, Leila, you are right. You are my better angel!'

'Oh, I am nothing to you, I know.'

'You shall be everything to me one day. I would to heaven that time were come ; but I reproach myself often with having gone so far——'

'You wish to go back—to have done with me?'

'No, darling, but I have fears that I cannot banish—fears not selfish, on my own account—fears for you, Leila.'

'What do you fear for me? What have I to fear from anyone? What do I care for anyone but you?'

'Ay, but the world, Leila—that is stronger than you or I either.'

'Not unless you choose to make it so ; you are my world.'

'Leila, you are a child ; you little know the power you set at defiance.'

'I know, I believe that men are slaves

to the world. What the world says of them makes or mars their happiness. I see now why you are changed to me.'

' I am not changed to you, Leila.'

' Yes, because a malicious newspaper writer chooses to cut me up, and a woman of rank, a married woman——'

' Hush! we will not talk about her, nor think about her any more ; give it time. I am going away in a few days ; I have many things to alter in my life—dangers to provide against that might affect my whole career—before I come back for a wife. I can make you no promise, Leila, but I am resolved that performance shall supply the place. We must wait awhile, and trust each other.'

' If I could only have your confidence !'

' In everything that concerns myself, you shall, darling ; all shall come right between us some day. I should be worse than a villain to mislead my sweet, innocent girl.'

I was half contented, with no power to complain ; my hands trembled beneath his kisses ; more than that he asked not of me. I could not tell at what moment I became aware that my grandmother was in the room. 'Then you are engaged?' she said, half-aloud. Arthur turned round upon her suddenly, releasing me.

'Mrs. Fortescue, it must not be so understood.'

'Sir, as an honorable man, with what intentions are you playing with this child?'

'My intentions are honorable; you will do us all the justice to assume they could be no other; but not matrimonial, for the present. I do not intend to marry for some years, and then, if I should be so fortunate as again to meet Miss Fortescue still free—but that is not likely; she will certainly have it in her power to choose one nearer to her in years, and in every way more suited to her. It is right that she should be unfettered in her choice. Leila must remain perfectly free.'

'That is plain enough to be thoroughly understood. Good morning, sir.' She curtsied, grasped my arm, and tottered out of the room, dragging me along with her. 'Leila,' he cried, pleadingly, 'you will bid me good-bye,' striving to reach my hand,

but she snatched it from him. I could not
have resised her will without restorting to
violence, from which I shrank. I had but
a look to give him ; but that look !

We were parted, and he was gone. I
watched him until he was out of sight, and
saw him looking back, myself unseen, then
sat down to weep my fill—I stole back to
the room where I had left him, where
there was no one now to watch me as I
sank down in my passion of woe, hearing
nothing, feeling nothing, until he was there,
come back again to feast upon my humiliation and weakness, Ah no! he caught
me in his arms, and then—and then—he
tore himself away with one last kiss, and
the indescribable low murmur ' My own,
my own,' of a love that can be felt, not
told.

CHAPTER VIII.

OR NOT AT ALL.

HE would write to me, surely, I thought; he did not, though months went by, and a rumor reached us that he was ere long to fill a high post in India. As days went on the chill of despair entered into my heart. I felt as if all was over between us.

Does a man reflect when he gives way to his fancy for a young girl, not taking thought at the time for the stronger motives that must in the end sway him back from his passing preference—does a man consider how awfully he compromises her, if not before the outer world, yet surely with that small inner round of her nearest relatives, her home, her actual daily life,

where it is far worse to be pitied and
despised ?   I did not show what I felt,
while my grandmother—having first bitterly
blamed me for what we had both tried
and failed in—sought to comfort me after
her fashion.   ' It was a case that cured
itself,' she said ; ' the man evidently never
cared for you, and there's an end of it.
Of course, you don't care any more than he
did, being the daughter of a much greater
man—if your father had lived——'   And so
the proud old lady reasoned on my feelings as though they must be the same as
her own.

I thought she wronged Arthur, that her
want of patience, if not mine, was to blame
for our defeat ; it was borne in upon me
with stronger conviction day by day, that
Arthur was fettered by some imbroglio
which he could not in a moment shake off,
that he was making efforts, only to be
effective with time, to work himself clear,
and through all, doing his best to act
honorably towards me.   One thing I not
only believed but knew—he had loved
me.

I was expected to join in reprobation of

him, to believe every impossible slander
that the good folk of Stormouth were not
slow to devise or circulate against him;
such stories as crop up in the London
clubs concerning every great character
prominently set in the world's eye, and are
eagerly caught up and detailed (with addi-
tions) by the envious and malicious, by
way of compensation to themselves for
their own inferiority of nature. Lady
Diana, it was said, and openly reported,
was in fact Arthur's mistress, had been so
for years, with the connivance of Sir John
Hope Trevor; the two men finding it their
interest to keep close friends on political
grounds, the husband conveniently shut
his eyes to what he must know, and the
couple were invited everywhere to meet
Arthur; to festivities, public and private,
on visits to noblemen's houses—Stormouth
Park, to wit—society by general consent
blinking with complacent eyes at the
illustrious sinner, as well as at the frail wife
of a too easy husband.

Had they said but half as much I should
have believed more; as it was I hated the
woman, but only trembled for Arthur.

Putting that and that together, the vile conclusions drawn by slanderers, and the facts known only to myself connected with the ring—oh, how it stung me to think he wore that on his finger still!—when all was said, I did not believe it was a case of guilt, although my instinct told me that woman was keeping him from me. Nothing could persuade me otherwise than that she it was who gave and pledged him to wear the ring, and if so, judging from his words and actions, he lay within her danger rather than within her power, and from this would it not be the nobler part, with my true, deep love, to strive for his rescue, casting aside the fear of evil consequences to me only?

It was better that I should do anything than calmly sit down and die, and let him go to perdition body and soul through her, my enemy. I knew he loved me. If I could but see him! How? He was in London now, I far away, where he was not likely to seek me out again ; alas, I felt sure of that! In London, where I knew not a human being—yes, one, out of his sphere and mine, but a kindly soul he had brought me in contact with, Mrs. Heathcote, the actress. I had the will, I must find the way, the means, the excuse for a short absence from home. I must set my face towards London, seek out Mrs. Heathcote, ask her countenance and protection, for want of better, make myself known to Arthur, see him, speak to him but once, if never to meet again in the course of our lives. All this flashed upon me together in one moment; it took many days of wretchedness and hesitation before it grew into shape, and I was resolved how the thing should be done, but then, never wavering, I held to my purpose, and bore it through.

There was no one I could take into my confidence or ask to be a companion of my journey. I must go alone, and this without my grandmother's consent, which I knew it would be useless to ask, but I made every endeavor, in taking my own course, to give her the least possible pain.

I wrote a letter, to be found by her after I was gone, in these words :

'MY DEAREST GRANNIE,

'I am leaving you for a short time, for a reason that you shall know hereafter, and, I trust, approve. Within a month at farthest I shall either return, or if, for a great object, my longer absence be required, I shall tell you all and act no further without your consent, which I implore of you to forgive my doing now, and not to fret. I shall take care of myself, as you have taught me to do, and have plenty of money to bring me back home, so do not trouble about me, Grannie dear, it is all for the best.

'Your loving child,'

'LEILA FORTESCUE.'

This I folded, with many tears, and left on a little table by her bed, where she was sure to find it on awaking in the morning. I had kissed her the night before, which I seldom did, for she never encouraged my caresses, and scarce seemed to know what to think of such unwonted tenderness, but my heart was full at parting with her; nothing could have driven me to so desperate a step, but the instinctive conviction that the worst I could possibly meet, being up and doing, would be less terrible to me than to sit still where I was and do nothing. I had not told Grannie a single falsehood to excuse myself.

Very early in the morning I arose and dressed for my journey. I could take nothing with me beyond what I could carry on my arm; money I had of my own, sufficient, with prudence, to fear no ship-wreck of my project on that score. Unheard by anyone in the house, I un-barred a window, and, slipping through the garden, let myself out into the road, and made my way in great haste to catch an early train for London. I was in much fear lest Grannie should wake before her time, pursue me, and stop my journey; if she slept till half-past seven, her usual hour, I should be miles away in the swift express, before an alarm could be raised to inter-cept my journey. Having no luggage to detain me on my arrival, I could escape from the station unnoticed, before any telegraphic action could be made effectual against me. Indeed, I do not believe poor Grannie ever thought of that, though, in my guilty fear, I clung close by two young ladies and their father, who travelled in the next carriage to me, wishing to appear as one of their party until I was able to lose myself in the crowd.

It was evening after my long travel, yet I did not dare to stop many minutes at the Great Western Station, where, if anywhere, search was likely to be made for me. Somehow, I was got into a cab, and directed the man to leave me at a station nearer the Strand, where I expected to lie *perdue* till the next morning, when I could seek out Mrs. Heathcote. How I dreaded that night alone in London, the first time I ever set foot within the mighty and terrible city! I dared not face any hotel. In the railway waiting-room, I felt as safe as I could be anywhere, and it was nobody's business to turn me out.

At eight o'clock in the morning I took a cup of tea and a bun, and having made such slight sacrifices to the Graces as time and place allowed, set out for the Strand, in a cab as before, giving my directions to be set down at the theatre where I knew Mrs. Heathcote was a member of the com-

pany. The man, after a long stare, whispered, confidentially, ' Stage door, miss ?'
' Yes,' I replied quickly, and in fear of
being overheard by some one who might
report the fact to my disadvantage, having
evidently acquired a special interest in
cabby's eyes.

He set me down at the stage door, and
volunteered his assistance in calling out
the porter to meet me after I had paid
him. He waited, as if curious to learn the
result of the interview. The porter looked
at me very hard, evidently drawing conclusions to my disadvantage, as having no
business there at that unreasonable hour.
' Rehearsal at half-past ten, miss, if you go
on as hextra lady,' he said, pragmatically
pointing with his finger to a paper posted
up inside his door, whereon was written
the correct date of that day, the hour he
indicated, and the words, ' Supers and
extra ladies '—inexplicable to any sense of
mine. All I knew was, it was but nine
o'clock, and I was not wanted, and the
whole aspect of the place, from the dingy
little pocket hole, where the porter made
his peculiar retreat, to the dark recesses

dimly perceptible beyond, was indescribably shocking to my feelings.

'I am a friend of Mrs. Heathcote's,' I took heart of grace and said: 'I am just come to town, and want to call upon her; will you please give me her address?'

'We don't give no private addresses of none of our ladies and gentlemen to nobody on no account, nohow. Them's our rules at this theatre, miss.'

'But I want to see Mrs. Heathcote. What am I to do?'

'If you'll come in the evening at half-past six—she's sure to be here—I'll take in your name to her dressing-room.'

'What! not before half-past six?'

'It may be just a chance that she'd look in through the day for her letters. Will you like to leave your name?'

"Letters! Then her letters come here, although you will not give her address? I should like to leave a letter for her."

'Oh, certainly, miss! You can write it here, if you like. I'll give you what you want.'

He did so. I wrote a hurried note, and

saw it placed in an alphabetical frame, hung up on the wall, beneath the letter H.

I was in haste to return to the railway station, to wait there until Mrs. Heathcote should come to me, as my note begged her to do. I felt out of place where I was, liable to be mistaken for some inferior *employée* hanging about the theatre. What would Arthur think of me, were he to pass by and surprise me ? I shrank into a corner at the bare idea. True, I had acted with him, but with a difference, in an assembly room, not a theatre, no such profane institution being tolerated at Stormouth, and in such ideas had I been brought up : with some inconsistency, I now threw mysel upon the good-nature of an actress as my only friend in need.

As I turned to take myself off, I was confronted on the narrow threshold by a face I knew.

'Oh, our stage manager, miss," said the porter.

'You here, my dear ?' said Mr. Heathcote, recognising me, with much surprise. But his style of address took me aback. ' My dear,' by inveterate habit as a stage manager, came from him quite naturally, but I fear made me blush at the awkwardness of my position.

'I wanted to see Mrs. Heathcote,' I said, constraining myself.

'Oh, my wife will be delighted. Go for a cab, Tom. I'll stop here for you. A private young lady we knew down in Cornwall. Send her off to the wife ; they'll understand each other.'

So it was settled, and under observation of half a score of the ubiquitous 'boy' species, among whom I seemed to excite a deep interest, I was handed into a cab *en route* for Mrs. Heathcote's lodgings.

What a world's wonder she made of me ! It was very painful to listen to her exclamations of astonishment at every word of explanation she drew from me. I would not tell her the whole truth, and she baulked at my half confidences, but kindly agreed to all my requests. It was arranged that I should have a room in the same house with her, and the use of her drawing-room for any visitors I wanted to see, some such I said there were. I had avoided mentioning Arthur's name.

'And now,' she resumed, 'I want you
to tell me what brought you up to London
all alone? Is it a fit of stage fever?—mad
to act? Is that it?'

'Well, no, but could I have the chance
to act if I wished?'

This was said half seriously. All else
failing, I might yet be glad of such a career
being open to me; it would be better that
motive should be attributed to my flight
both by the Stormouth gossips and my
grandmother, anything to hide the truth
from them! Mrs. Heathcote thought twice
before she answered me.

'Act—yes, I dare say you could be
taught to act. There's a good deal of stuff
in you.' She eyed me as if taking measure
of my qualities. 'But you've everything
to learn. You were not such a bad Desdemona for quite a novice, and after two
years' hard work you might do. But, bless
the child! you'd be sick of it in two weeks!
And your singing voice would be sure to
go—and such a pity!'

'My singing voice?'

'Yes, certain to be lost, "speaking up,"
as we call it, destroys all your high notes
for singing.'

' I did not know——'

' Of course not, how should you know anything about it ?   My dear, if you want to take to a profession, be a singer, nothing else ; besides, it's much more respectable than the stage.   Very few of us can hold the position we deserve.   My lord some-body's mistress is always stopping the way.'

' Do bad women, then, please the public best ?'

' No, but they keep others out as long as they find the money to force themselves down the throat of the public, and are not found out.   Ten years ago a leading actress was supposed to be a woman of character ; now the contrary is the rule instead of the exception.'   I shuddered. ' There are not three actresses at our theatre that Mr. Heathcote would admit inside this house.   We meet them in business, that's all.   Oh, you're quite safe as a young girl under my wing.'

There needed no more bespattering of her own nest ; the sight I had had of the ' behind the scenes' was sufficient to dis-gust my fastidiousness.   Neither would I risk any hurt to my singing voice, which I had already learnt to prize beyond all other earthly possessions, as the lever that might yet raise my little world into a higher sphere, could I but find the proper vantage point to work from !

I had come, however, to find out Arthur —to see him, to warn him—and with nervous sensitiveness I shrunk from revealing my intent to any mortal ear, hard as I found it, unaided and uncounselled, to shape the way of our meeting. Unless I made some endeavors to seek him out, I might remain in London my life long unknown to him. On the chance that we might be brought together, without any palpable effort of mine, I asked Mrs. Heathcote to sit with me in the Park, morning or afternoon, whenever she could, and there I watched and waited, day after day, at least for a distant sight of him. This was denied me, though royalty, wealth, and fashion spread all their glamours before my young, impressionable eyes. To me the sight was the most wonderful I had ever seen or dreamed of out of a fairy tale, How I smile on recalling my simplicity now ! At first I was fascinated, then I sunk into the

deepest depression, crushed, as it were, in
spirit, by the sight of the great pageant of
the world's vanity, rolling and rolling on
without a thought or a look for the poor
mortality that lay beneath the chariot
wheels ; not a human being there that
knew me or that I could name, among
those thousands upon thousands !   Why
had I left my home ?   I was a stranger
here.

A presentiment flashed upon me : might
I not one day conquer for myself a place
among that haughty throng ?   A prouder
place than the accidents of birth and wealth
can confer by right ? might I not work my
own way up by dint of courage and perse-
verance, added to the gifts of genius I felt
were mine ?   I had heard of such things,
how the talent which in a woman had been
looked upon as a clog and a hindrance in
obscure country life, in London became a
power in her weak hands, an instrument to
fortune and fame ! Yes, one day I would
make myself a name, through the rich
treasures that were in me of melody and
song ; and if this might be realized, why
not that other dearer hope ? To make my-

self worthy of my high-placed love, to be
accepted for my own merits, not by claim
of rank, to reach his side by a different
road to fame, to be lost in his greater light,
his love, his wife ! I must not dare to think
such thoughts, but bend my spirit to the
stern necessities that lay to my hand to
cope withal.

There was no other way, I must write
him a letter, ask him to come to me, un-
certain whether he would receive it, or, if he
did, when he would comply. I did not think
he could refuse me. I wrote and sent it to
his official address, with the words ' Private
and Personal ' by way of precaution against
the curiosity of profane clerks. Thus ran
my letter :

' Having heard no word from you for
several months, I should not know, but for
the public mention of your name, whether
or not you were among the living. I know
not whether you care to hear that I am so
still, but even if not, I feel I owe a duty to
one so great of heart, who has once shown
me kindness, and that is to warn you for
your own sake of a danger that threatens

you, through the malice of others. It is
such a matter as I could not write, but will
tell you all I know if yóu will see me for
once, here, where I am staying while in
London, with Mrs. Heathcote. Send a
line to·say when I may expect you, as in a
few days I shall return home, and after this
one interview I do not suppose that we
shall ever meet again ; none the less shall
I be, in memory of your former kindness,
for all my life your true friend,

'LEILA FORTESCUE.'

CHAPTER IX.

THE DESIRE ACCOMPLISHED.

I HAD kept the paper unblotted by any tear of mine. My honor I would hold safe, even though my life were wrung from me in the bitter drops I wept, as hot blood from my heart.

That secure, let the rest go!

Not so; I had won my hero to my feet.

Need I tell how I watched and listened for the postman on his round, as if my very existence hung upon his approaching knock, that passed and died away four times every day, or worse, battered at the door beneath on some other's behalf, but brought nothing for me? Two days passed thus, till my strange absence of mind drew remark from the few around me, and then, late in the afternoon, unannounced and unexpected, there was heard upon the stairs a step I knew; a knock at the drawing-room door, ' Come in,' from my companion, Mrs. Heathcote, and Arthur stood before me.

' I came the moment I received your letter,' he said; ' I have been down at Woolwich for two days; I would not wait to write and appoint an hour. I have come on chance of finding you, and am fortunate.'

I was much embarrassed at this discovery to Mrs. Heathcote of my having written to Arthur in the way I had done, and could find neither explanation nor reply. She at once took in the situation in its general bearings, and good-naturedly left the room. Arthur seemed in no hurry to learn what I had to tell him; he only caressed my hand, and said he was happy we met again. ' But this,' he added, ' is not the way you ought to be in London. Mrs. Heathcote is a very good woman in her way, but you have friends, surely—— ?'

'None in London,' I interrupted; 'very few anywhere.'

'And why did you come to London?'

'If you will not think ill of me, I will tell you all the truth.'

'I could never think ill of you. Tell me, Leila.'

'I came alone, and unknown to my best friend—my grandmother—for a short time only; I have promised to return in a few days. I came away to—to try and see you this once, for the sake of your own honor and high name, because I could not bear to listen any longer to the horrible things I heard them say of you, and I would sacrifice myself in any way to put an end to the cause.'

'The cause is very simple, Leila, but, I am afraid, the harder to cure. Every man with a name so much in the mouth of the world as mine, must expect to have dirt thrown upon his reputation. The less you believe of it, Leila, the kinder to me you will be, and, I hope, the nearer the truth.'

'But when one name is remarkably mixed up with yours to the injury of both, why do you not avoid the world's suspicion ? Why are you for ever meeting Lady Diana Hope Trevor, no matter where you go ?'

His brow grew dark, and the shadow of it fell upon my mind. 'Was she at Woolwich while you were there ?' I asked.

'She was. They had a ball, and could not help inviting her, nor could I refuse to go merely because she was there.'

'You danced with her ?'

'Yes, once.'

'But you danced with no one else ?'

'I was not expected to dance in general. Really, Leila, this is silly of you.'

'Trifles, straws show the way of the deepest current. When you met me at Stormouth, at the ball, you did not ask me to dance.'

'It would have made you too remarkable. I never dance, scarcely.'

'Except with Lady Diana ; you are not afraid of making her remarkable.'

'I should not do so. All the world knows we have been acquainted many years, since she and I were young.'

I shuddered at something in his tone.

'Since she and I were young'—perhaps
lovers.

'Leila, let there be no more of this
between us. There is one way to end it
all, and to make me happier than I have
ever been in my life—with you, Leila. I
do not yet see my course quite clear, but
time will bring it straight. There are
reasons which I cannot explain to you yet,
why I could not present my wife at court,
or elsewhere in England for a time, but in
a few months I expect my appointment in
India, and once this is settled, the difficulty
can be smoothed down. Would you consent to a secret marriage at once? and
then I shall be sure of you as my own.'

It came upon me like a thunderbolt;
sense and motion had been almost taken
away from me by the strong blow of joy.
I did not answer him.

'Leila,' he whispered, 'you love me—
do you love me? I know you do. There
is no other way but to be united now,
indissolubly. Once let this chance pass, and
we shall be separated—perhaps for ever.
You will consent to anything I wish? Is
it not so, Leila?'

'How can I deny you? You know well you can do with me anything you will; you will do nothing but what is honorable: but what do you mean by a secret marriage? Will it be in a church?'

'In church or by a clergyman, what does the place signify?'

'But my grandmother must know; I am under age; we must have her consent.'

'I do not think that will be requisite.'

'She would give it willingly, and keep our secret.'

'I had much rather she had it not to keep, for your sake as much as my own. Until I can take you away to India you must remain with her as usual; it is best that she know nothing until then.'

'So I shall not write to her about it?'

'Not on any account.'

'But Mrs. Heathcote, that I am staying with, she will be sure to find out——'

'She must not—you must look to that; she of all others must not know that I am anything to you but a friend.'

'I cannot imagine how we can be married
so secretly as that.'

'I cannot tell you at this moment;
but I pledge my honor and my soul to find
a way.'

'If I were to go home to my grandmother, you could follow me, and our
clergyman would make us safe, and never
tell a word to mortal, until the right
time came. I am sure he would, and
Grannie would be so happy!' I pleaded,
wavering in my hard attempt to meet his
will.

'Leila, that is impossible; what you ask
is the same as if you required me to cut off
my sword arm on the eve of battle. The
story would ooze out and ruin me. No,
Leila, if you love me, we must be married
in the best way I can settle it here; in a
few days you shall know how it can be
done, secretly and safely. I want you,
Leila, I cannot do without you now; but if
you will not trust me so far as I ask of you,
I must.'

I trembled and felt subdued to his
purpose. Was he not my head, my lord,
the guide and protector of my life and

honor ? to doubt of whom would be a crime, a sacrilege ?

'We shall be married, Leila, within a week—you will not cross me again, my own darling. I have enough—' He broke short, and was silent as to the rest.

'Anything—anything in the world you ask me,' I murmured, incoherently. 'Your own Leila I have been ever since the first hour we met. You can take me.'

My voice broke into inarticulate sobs : I was laid upon his breast, trembling with a great and fearful joy : his lips were upon my ear, whispering, 'My own love, kiss me ; will you not ?'

I did not dare, though he had taken many and many a kiss of me in those last few moments.

'Leila, you will kiss me as your husband ?'

I lifted my head a little and met those dark, resistless eyes that swayed me as it were my fate : he was smiling on my fear, in the delight of his heart ; the fond, loving smile, that brought back more than the charm of youth into that grandly chiselled face, almost divine in its tender beauty now.   It was bending lower and lower towards mine ; my soul rose to my lips with a sharp cry, and a wild clasp of lifted arms, as our lips met—oh, earth ! oh, life ! I could have died in his embrace.

CHAPTER X.

IS SWEET TO THE SOUL.

At last I had achieved my great happiness, the triumph that could not be taken away from me. I knew that nothing of what was to come could go beyond what I felt now : I had won it for myself by my true love and self-devotion, like the young Saracen maiden, who loved an English warrior, her father's captive, gained him his liberty, and then, when he had returned home and forgotten her perhaps, followed after him, alone and ignorant of his very language, found her way with one word— 'London'—to the great city where he lived, and wandering from street to street, with one other word only on her lips,—his name, 'Gilbert'—was found by him, and became his wife, the mother of Thomas-à-Beckett. How like to hers was now my story!

But, as Matilda-à-Beckett had to be properly instructed and christened before she sank her Oriental identity in that good English title, so in my case there was a host of preliminary obstacles to be got over. Three different times did Arthur come with a different plan to propose, and, as each involved more or less risk of discovery in the execution, he had to content himself finally with the choice of the least evil, which was, marriage by banns in a church remote in the city, and likely to be almost without congregation on the Sundays when the banns would be asked, as the holidays of Easter time would remove about half of the scanty dozen or score of parishioners who usually attended. A kind of disguise was found for the arrangement of Arthur's names, mine were sufficiently obscure to attract no notice. A store room for luggage was engaged on Arthur's behalf, so as to acquire for him the requisite status as a parishioner.

Sooth to say, neither I nor the church authorities showed ourselves hard to deal with : for my part, why should I ? Against another woman, a malicious enemy to both, I knew all Arthur's precautions were taken. From her snares and traps I had saved him by a generous compliance with his wishes, preferred before my own ; yes, I had so saved him, and had no hesitation in setting this, the higher duty, above any former tie or worldly prejudice that could condemn me. Was he not the same as my husband now ? As such I obeyed him, my honor being held as a part of his : as such I loved him well enough to marry him how he could, or to die for him.

Mrs. Heathcote began to have her suspicions, which were likely to prove rather inconvenient, in view of the short week's honeymoon, upon which Arthur insisted, so that our ingenuity was much taxed to defeat her curiosity. We were to be married at the end of the fortnight, singly and quietly to make our way, by nine in the morning, to the church appointed, and not till the next day, for fear of discovery, was I to set out, presumably

on my return home, but, in fact, to stop a
week at Weymouth on the way, Arthur being at the station beforehand to join me and
travel together. This intent Mrs. Heathcote did her endeavors (unconsciously) to
frustrate by declaring she would see me off
herself, and my luggage, properly labelled
for Stormouth, into the train. We were
obliged to devise a meeting at the station,
quasi accidental. Arthur would say he
was going to Weymouth for his post-
Easter retirement out of town, and assume
to himself the charge of my luggage, while
leaving Mrs. Heathcote to choose my place
in the ladies' compartment, to be vacated
by me at the first station we stopped at, as
the worst of our case, if Mrs. Heathcote
should keep her vigilant eye upon us till
the departing puff of the engine, as she
threatened to do.

I did not dare to write a word to Grannie,
lest if she knew I was in London, she
might set some inquiry on foot, which,
reaching Mrs. Heathcote, or anyone else
who might have heard of my being with
her, would have ruined all ; it would be six
weeks after I left home before I could

return, and I had to look for many chidings, and worse, much sorrow for my truant disposition, from my poor grandmother, who was sure to torment herself and me with a world of suspicions—any cause but the right one—which would content her so well if she knew—would be assigned for my strange wanderings. Probably, on the score of my residence with Mrs. Heathcote, I should be branded with the conviction of a passion for the stage, which, even worse than such for a man, would compromise my already suspected name with the Stormouth folk. Let it be as it would, in six months Arthur would take me with him to India as his wife.

It was impossible to keep Mrs. Heathcote from wondering at me. I had but one dress, a handsome travelling suit : I required another—I thought it must be white, to be married in. This I had to buy somehow in Mrs. Heathcote's presence, for I could not venture out shopping in London alone, all my pluck and resolution being held in reserve for the desperate final adventure of getting to the church to be married. So Mrs. Heathcote took me to

a shop she recommended for any purchases
I required, but as I was going home so
soon, she did not see the necessity of just
what I could not do without, and especially
set her face against the white dress, as the
most useless I could encumber myself with
travelling. 'It would make me conspicuous,'
she said, 'and moreover look soiled after a
day's wear, while a neat *écru* would be
much more suitable and becoming.' I had
to be obstinate and stick to the white, and
then there were coloured ribbons to be
removed.

'Have black,' suggested Mrs. Heathcote.

'No, white; they must be white,' I
blurted.

'White silk bows and sash, do you
mean, to wear by daylight in the street?
My dear, you'll be stared at as if you had
a hundred heads on; nonsense!'

'But can't I have all white in some way?
I don't care how, but I have a fancy for a
dress all white; my grandmother told me
she used to wear all white when she was a
girl.'

'That's half a century ago: girls don't

go about in broad daylight with white dresses now—not with white silk certainly,' then, appealing to the authority of the dressmaker : ' Did you ever make one of the kind ? I am sure you never did.'

' Well, only for young ladies going to a wedding,' was the meek reply, ' we have made them with muslin sash and bows, the same as this dress, sometimes, but they are not often required ; ladies prefer coloured or black ribbon.'

I contrived to seize upon the opening for a compromise ; the dress was to be one entire fabric of soft opaque white. Next I had to procure, with as little observation as possible, some few dainty articles to do duty for the usual paraphernalia of a bride, as patterns, I said, I wanted them ; Mrs. Heathcote objected that they could not be properly copied without taking to pieces, and being spoiled, and recommended paper patterns instead. I had to shut my ears to her arguments and take my own way.

' What extraordinary fancies girls will take when they go out shopping and put on a spurt !' was her opinion of me.

Then for my white gloves.

'Never, except for a wedding,' cried Mrs. Heathcote. 'My dear, you're not going to be married!'

The damsels of the counter smiled at one another, they evidently suspected I was, which Mrs. Heathcote observing, took offence both with them and me.

'I want a nice pair of white gloves,' I said, 'because I never can get the size that fits me in Stormouth, except I order them weeks beforehand ; they do not keep my number, and they send for them to London, so I may as well get them myself while I am here.'

Little hands to the rescue! I carried off the gloves triumphantly, and Mrs. Heathcote carried off me ; evidently our day's business together had set her a-thinking, none the less that she 'put her tongue a little in her heart.'

Next day was Sunday, the 'first time of asking' it was to be, and it seemed to me as if the sun rose with another light than that of common day ; as the hours rolled on, and no strange accident befel to cross their course, no shadow of impending fate went

backwards on the dial of time, no moon
nor star suffered unnatural change, when
the evening of that morning made the
Sabbath day, then did the union that day
heralded become real to my perception,
and certain to my hope ; in a brief fortnight, thus long, and no longer, was I to
be the I that I was, an unwedded maid ;
then should I be changed, another, though
the same, to become a part of him, no more
myself only, his, not my own, his wife.
Truly it was a great and wonderful thing
to think of, a tremendous revolution in my
little life, like a death and a resurrection ;
a great joy and shuddering got hold upon
me, as on one with bandaged eyes
tottering upon the threshold of another
world ! His love was to be the hereafter
of my soul, which he should gather unto
him !

On the Monday at breakfast time Mrs.
Heathcote came down in a handsome
black silk dress, in lieu of her morning
merino toilet, usual for receiving her
pupils ; she was a noted teacher of the
dramatic art, no less than an able exponent
of the same. Monday being one of her

special teaching days when she would have much 'business' to go through in course of instruction to young actresses, her pupils, this silk dress, of which she was particularly chary on such occasions, struck her husband as a peculiarity, of which he took it into his head to enquire the reason on her following him down to breakfast. She answered, putting a letter into his hand.

'Look what I received by this morning's post, it was brought up to me after you were gone down stairs, being marked immediate. You read it. I haven't made out half the words—only I'm to expect her at eleven o'clock; I must put off Miss Tudor's lesson in consequence.'

Mr. Heathcote took and read the letter.

'DEAR MADAM,

'Will you assist me in a most embarrassing situation? I am to play Marie de Fontanges to-morrow fortnight, and my usual dramatic adviser, Mrs. Cibber, has gone to the country on a starring engagement, so that I have really nobody to

coach me in the part.   I know nothing
about it, but I hear it is a splendid one,
and I ought to make a great hit with it,
being just my style, so I want you to
teach it to me, as I hear you are the best
in the profession—you and Mrs. Cibber.
I shall want to take a long lesson every
day, or two lessons, or more, if we can
find the time, together.   I shall call upon
you early to-morrow—say eleven o'clock,
hoping to catch you at that hour—and we
can begin then, if convenient to you.
There is no time to be lost if I am to do
you and myself credit.

      ' I remain, dear Mrs. Heathcote,

          ' Very truly yours,

              ' DIANA HOPE TREVOR.'

    This being dated Sunday, within another
hour she would be here.

CHAPTER XI.

'TWIXT CUP AND LIP.

ONE hour, and my enemy would stand in this very room, talking to the woman who was now to me as a friend, discovering me, guessing, conjecturing, I knew not what, perhaps the very truth itself, which, as my life, I was bound to guard against her envious eyes. I had to plead with Mrs. Heathcote for my all, and without telling her so.

'Lady Diana is coming here,' I said, 'then I must keep away out of sight, and I beg of you, do not mention me at all, and if she does, pray tell her nothing of me.'

'I should not think of such a thing. Why, what could I tell her of you?'

'She must not know that I am in London.'

'Why not? she has no right to find fault with your coming to town as well as everybody else.'

'She must not know why; she must not hear that I am with you; she might make a story out of it.'

'Out of me? Nonsense, she might think you wanted to take to the stage. You would be ashamed of that, young lady.'

'Not in itself.   I should not like it to be set down that I had tried the stage and failed.'

'But you didn't; you've never done anything of the kind.'

'Don't you remember that spiteful attack in the paper?'

'The *Empress*? Oh, yes, that was rather severe upon you.'

'That was Lady Di's contrivance, I'm convinced, to destroy my chance of acting again.'

'I don't know that; the *Empress* was safe to cut you up in any case.'

'But why—when they knew nothing about me?'

'That's just the reason; you're not a friend of theirs.'

'But they told a dozen falsehoods of me.'

'You don't expect they would stop at the truth? The editor is a woman, one of the strong minded, goes in for woman's rights; what would you have? Can't you see the feminine style? a succession of pin thrusts! Now, a man's abuse would hit wider of the mark.'

'My grandmother would never consent to my appearing in public again after that article.'

'My dear, it can't do you any harm; nobody reads the *Empress*, except for the fashion plates.'

'Lady Diana had it written: she is jealous of anyone—of me——'

'I think you may say that, my dear.'

'She is jealous of—my acting.'

'Perhaps she pays you that compliment, and another as well—you are too young, too attractive—to one gentleman, at least.

'May I trust you, Mrs. Heathcote?—can you keep a secret for me? will you promise, if I tell you what it was that brought me to London——?'

'Oh, I thought you were mad for the stage. Wasn't that it?'

'It was not.'

'Singular, then, your coming to me.'

'I came to you as a friend. I have no friend in London, except—except him, and I did not know beforehand how he would take it when I came. Promise me, on your solemn word, you will tell no mortal what brought me—not even your husband must know.' He had left the room before our conversation.

'Not even my husband? Well, that is a secret!'

'I cannot tell you unless you promise.'

'Well, I promise. Come.'

'Arthur was the cause—he only. I came to see him—to—I must not say any more.'

'If that's all you've got to tell me I'm sorry I promised to make any secret of it. I knew that much before, by the use of my own eyes, and was quite free to tell any-one I pleased.'

'Oh, but you will not! That would be the same as if you were to kill me.'

'My child, you take it so to heart! I see you have a heart that will hurt you all your life through. There is nothing

whatever in the case that you should look
on it that way. You have done no harm,
I hope, in coming to me.'

'No, but there are things I cannot tell
you.'

'I understand. Be careful of yourself,
my child, and do not believe all a man
says to you; men say anything when they
have a point to gain with a girl like you.
I will do all I can for you, even without
being much in your confidence. I shall
not repeat anything you have said—no,
not to my husband, nor speak of you at all
to Lady Diana.'

'But if she questions you? She may be
coming on purpose.'

'I don't think that likely; but I shall
say I don't know anything about you. In
business it is always allowable to say we
don't know, when people ask inconvenient
questions.'

I kept close in my own room all the
time I knew my enemy was in the house;
when she was gone, at the end of two and
a half mortal hours, and the door closed
after her, I crept down, half afraid lest the
creaking of a stair beneath my light foot-

step might work as a spell to recall her.
I stood at the door of the drawing-room,
hesitating.

'Come in, my dear, the coast is quite
clear, no enemy in sight,' said Mrs. Heathcote, laughing at my trepidation; 'we've
had a long lesson, and I hope my lady is
content with herself; I should not be, I
know, if I had to work like that only for
one performance.'

'You have been more than two hours
giving her a lesson.'

'Oh, that's nothing! She comes at ten
to-morrow for another two hours, and every
day for a fortnight. It seems these
amateurs have their rehearsals in the afternoon, so she comes to me early. She
wanted me to dine with her, and go on in
the evening rehearsing her part, but I'm
playing just now, so of course, that's out
of the question.'

'She wants lessons both morning and
evening?'

'Morning, noon, and night rehearsing.
She wouldn't do another mortal thing if
human patience could stand it Mine
could not, though I get a guinea an

hour.   She's as good as a second engagement to me for the fortnight.'

'You have to teach her everything?'

'Teach her! Word by word, parroting. Not a blessed idea has she of the part; and as to business, she knows less than a utility novice could teach her, until she has gone through everything with me over and over and over again.   In general I tell people two or three times the same thing, and then, if they don't take it, I leave them to themselves, but that would not do with her, she would raise a laugh at every line.   She must make it worth somebody's while to teach her or she could not act.   Mrs. Cibber must have made a pot of money out of that lady pupil.'

'She will be sick of her part before she plays it : don't you think it a bad plan to make acting such a cut and dry task?'

'My dear, I'm an artist; I don't care what trouble I take, so there's an end worth gaining, no more than you would with your singing : I could understand any labor to appear before the public, that's fame, but to play one night for one's own friends !—well, some people are mad.'

Knowing the time that Lady Diana was to come next day, I wrote to Arthur by way of precaution :

'For a reason that I shall explain when we meet, you must be cautious in coming to see me here ; to-morrow afternoon all will be safe, but on no account must you come from ten to twelve o'clock in the morning. Keep it secret that you visit at the house at all ; I shall always let you know before-hand, when it is safe for you to come. Hoping to meet to-morrow, ever your own,

'LEILA.'

This sent I was able to close my eyes somewhat, but not much, that night : again I had to lie *perdue*, like a bird afraid to stir out of her nest, knowing that the hawk is overhead, disporting unconscious of her existence, but none the less ready for a pounce down upon her, if she give the chance. I knew that another pupil was to follow Lady Diana, therefore I remained upstairs till Mrs. Heathcote called me down at half past-one.

'I beg your pardon, my dear,' she said;
I've actually had no time to think of you
till now; such a "fussification" as we've
had! but it's always the way with amateurs,
something essential is sure to fall through,
or be forgotten till the last moment.'

'What's the matter with Lady Diana
now? Is she not happy?'

'Not at all; at least, she was not till I
made her so; they had nobody to play
her waiting-maid. Just fancy!'

'An unenviable position, I should say,
either in jest or earnest.'

'A very pretty little part; must be young
and attractive to look it, and they thought
they had it filled all right; but this is a
public charity performance, so the young
lady's papa would not allow her to appear,
and that's all off.'

'Then the part will have to be cut out?'

'No such thing! I told Lady Diana
Miss Tudor could play it. She is studying
for the stage with me, but has never
appeared. I don't care about my pupils
playing with amateurs in general, but
this is an exceptional case—everything will
be properly done.'

Here was a blow! Miss Tudor, who knew me by sight and by name, brought into juxtaposition with Lady Diana. 'Miss Tudor will play with them?' I gasped out.

'To be sure she will! Five guineas and all expenses paid. I told her never to play with amateurs unless they made it worth her while; but Lady Diana jumped at the girl. I introduced them to one another, and it's all arranged.'

An odd idea struck me: 'I wonder how much the charity will benefit by it all?'

'The charity?—who ever heard of amateurs caring for charity, except as a cloak to hide their vanity? Charity's just a pretence for acting; that's all. I dare say they'll have a splendid house for that small place; two hundred pounds, perhaps, but then the expenses will run up. If the charity gets fifty pounds, they'll think they've done wonders. In most of these cases, the charity gets nothing at all; I think it's very wrong.'

'And so do I, and I am very unhappy that Miss Tudor has anything to do with it ; she knows me, she will be sure to tell. Oh, could you not prevent—find some one else ? 'Tis nothing to her to play with these amateurs.'

'·Nothing ?—five guineas, and her first appearance on any stage ? not that I should reckon it as a first appearance.'

' It is everything in this world to me, to keep myself out of Lady Diana's power or knowledge until I leave London.'

' I never thought of such a thing. I am sorry, but it can't be helped now; everything's settled. I'll tell Miss Tudor not to mention your name ; I think I can depend upon her. But what a ' closet lock and key of villainous secrets' you are making of me, my young lady !'

Late that afternoon came Arthur. I knew by his light spring up the stairs that he was in high spirits ; he came as the eagle, exulting in the renewal of youth his young love had put into his life—his very soul overflowing in exuberant gaiety from his lips. How could I find the heart to throw a damp upon our joy ?

' At last, my darling, at last ! As many kisses as I want, if that could be ; they are

all my own now. Our banns were asked
last Sunday. Hush and hurrah ! Nobody
suspects us.'

' I hope not—but I at least am in misery
at the risks I run.'

' Risks ! What risks ? You would not
let me come this morning, or you would
have had the good news before.'

' Arthur, you don't knów, but I must
tell you, though I hate the sound of her
name. Lady Diana comes here every day,
to take lessons with Mrs. Heathcote.'

' Nonsense ! She take lessons ! Why,
she's a better actress herself than Mrs.
Heathcote in anything.'

' Don't you think such a thing—a parrot,
a piece of monkey tricks ; she has to learn
her part like her A B C. Mrs. Heathcote
says she only exists for the sole purpose of
rehearsing.'

' What a passion for acting she must
have ! Well, that ought to content you, if
you believe that a woman is capable of
only one passion at a time ; if her whole
existence is absorbed in acting, my darling
little girl should be the last to complain.'
He said this with a roguish smile, that

failed to confirm my confidence in him.

'Masculine vanity! I declare I believe you are piqued that I should think another woman does not care for you; but I do not think so, sir. I believe her acting is all a trick to entangle you.'

'Well, then, she gives herself a world of trouble about nothing. Does she come here every day, did you say?'

'Every morning for two or three hours.'

'Then I must not come so often, to draw remarks and trouble upon you. What is she studying now?'

'Marie de Fontange; she plays it on Monday week, the day of our marriage.'

'That day, of all others! I have heard of this performance to come off; in fact, she has invited me to be present.'

'But you cannot on that day!'

'Why not? You forget we do not set off till the next morning, and it is vital to me to lull suspicion of anything extra- ordinary being connected with my going out of town. I am half sorry now I did not take Mrs. Fortescue into our confidence; I could have gone down and married you at home, by special license. That might have been the safest plan after all, but there's no help for it now.'

'May I tell Mrs. Heathcote?—and she will help me, I know, to keep away suspicion from others.'

'Not for the world; she must know nothing.'

'I am afraid she knows too much, or not enough already; she remarks how I blush and tremble at your name. I cannot help it, when I know we are so soon to be—I cannot hide that I do care for you!'

'My darling, innocent girl! pretend to care for me only a little—that's the way when you care very much—it is safer than trying to look as if you did not care at all.'

'I wish I could care for you only a little; it would be better for me, and just as well for you. I care for you too much, or you would not have the heart to give me such cruel pain—to spend the evening of our wedding day with—with her.'

'Come, you're afraid she will unmarry us: is that it?'

'Don't laugh at my misery; I cannot bear it, when you are making me do what

I know to be wrong, too! Mrs. Heathcote ought to know the truth, and then I should have one friend, at least, I could depend upon to help me through—indeed I want it.'

'My darling child, you must let me think for you in this; you cannot know what I know, and it is my right to direct you as your guide and protector through life. You are not fit to deal with a thorough woman of the world, so leave her to me, and I will do all for the best. Think, you are little more than a child. Trust me, darling.'

Still less could I resist his caresses than his words, and so gave up my own judgment, feeling still that it was better than his, as the true, right instinct of a child may be wiser than man's reason. My youth was coming against me now! alas, so it seemed! I was too young for him!

CHAPTER XII.

THERE'S MANY A SLIP.

THE day after this interview I received a letter from Arthur :

'MY DEAREST LOVE,

'For your sake, as much as for my own, and to disarm suspicion, I am leaving town for these next ten days ; at the end of that time I shall return to claim your hand, having left all in safe course towards that end. If you are sorry for what you have done, or feel any natural hesitation in entrusting the peace and happiness of your young life to one not worthy of you, it is not too late to retreat ; do as you will, I shall ever remain yours with the truest and deepest affection,

'ARTHUR.'

Alas ; he knew me too well, and was too
sure of me, his own, heart, soul and life, or
he would never thus have put me to the
proof! What change could come must come
from himself ; for all such was to me impossible ; he knew it, I knew he knew it ; what
more could I but strive to banish the doubt
that rose unbidden, the mistrust of him I
loved, hateful as the infidel murmur against
heaven's truth, rising up in the heart when
the power of darkness casts a shadow of
death and hell upon the believer's soul !
Another Sunday came, and he was absent ;
this was the second time our names were
asked, now safely over. Once more, and
all would be well ; this confidence was
growing in me ! I did not go out, not even
to church, being fearful the very stones
would observe me. Morning and afternoon I shut myself in my room for fear of
visitors who might talk about me—not, as
it proved, without good cause to fear.

Mrs. Heathcote was going out to seven
o'clock dinner at Lady Diana's, her husband was bound for stage-land. When they
were both gone, I meditated to glide
downstairs and post a letter to Arthur un-

observed. It was nearly six, and I had begun to watch and listen for their going out, when a quick knock came to the door, and the agitation of some unexpected visitor made itself felt from the drawing-room with a stir and commotion that sounded through the whole house. I found it most prudent not to move until Mrs. Heathcote's strong voice, and the clapping of the hall-door, gave indication of the intruder's departure. Then, oh, how my heart leaped up in my throat as Mrs. Heathcote screamed to me rather than called : 'Miss Fortescue, Miss Fortescue, where are you ? Are you upstairs ? Come down ; I want to speak to you. What's become of the girl ? Leila Fortescue !'

I came down, shaking in every fibre of my frame.

'Miss Fortescue, you're going to be married—don't deny the truth : I've discovered it all ; that's what you came to me for, and you never told me. Oh, what a deep girl you are ! and so young, too !'

No reply from me : she had not mentioned *him*, and I had presence of mind enough to hear the end of the accusation before I would commit myself, perhaps to something that no accuser could prove against me. Provoked by my silence she went on :

'You shall not stir out of this house to-night.'

'I do not want to, Mrs. Heathcote.'

'Miss Fortescue, you are an awful girl! To-morrow I shall communicate with your friends, and tell them I wash my hands of all responsibility. You want to make some bad, disgraceful marriage !'

What a relief! she was all in the dark, evidently. I became the questioner.

'No such thing, Mrs. Heathcote, I assure you on my honor as a lady. Who told you so ? and what have you heard of me ?'

'Miss Tudor has just been here, and told me she heard your banns asked to-day, with her own ears, in that out-of-the-way church—what did she call it ? I forget. She's a very religious girl, and she took it into her head to attend church this morning, and went to that church, for the sake of the walk, she said, and because there would be plenty of room there. I can't say whether she had heard any whisper of what was going on ; she heard your banns for the second time of asking.'

' Did she say so ?'

' Yes, heard your name, Leila Fortescue ; she could not be mistaken, she said, and now what are you going to do with your-self, young lady ? Something very bad, or you would not want to be married by banns ; no respectable people ever are.'

'You are all in the wrong,' I said, smiling with involuntary triumph at my noble choice, ' but I cannot tell you any more now than you can find out for your-selves.'

I could see or hear from Arthur before the next Sunday, and doubted not that he would find a way to bring me through this dilemna.

' I shall forbid the banns,' cried Mrs. Heathcote, ' I shall not allow you to be married, unless you give me satisfactory reasons before the day comes, and show me your grandmother's consent. Why, you're a child ! not seventeen ; you don't know what you are doing. Can't you wait and be properly married ? If the man

means well, he can find no fault with that.
Whom do you want to marry? Mr.
Arthur, Miss Tudor thought, was the
name: perhaps some married man, taking
you in under a false one. I don't know
any Mr. Arthur.'

Anything rather than that she should
suspect the truth without his permission!
I have called him 'Arthur' in this narra-
tive; she did not know him by that name,
but by his usual style and title only. We
had contrived that 'Arthur' should have
prominent place in the asking of banns, so
as to mystify the congregation, no heed
being likely to be taken of my unnoted
name, and all jumbled together into a
string of undefined pronunciation, it was
by the worst of ill-luck that any attention
had been attracted thereto. I felt I was
safe so long, and so long only, as no one
detailed the circumstances to Lady Diana.
She would know the love-name 'Arthur,'
I thought, only too well.

'Mrs. Heathcote,' I said, 'I will venture
to promise you shall know and approve
of all by this day week; but upon the
condition that Lady Diana Hope Trevor

knows nothing, hears nothing in the mean-
time ; I know her evil mind to ruin me as
a rival.'

Had I betrayed my secret ? Mrs.
Heathcote said, 'Oh!' a light evidently
breaking in upon her, which I had not
intended to expose to view ; then, after a
pause : ' Well, my dear, perhaps you are
in the right after all ; you're just the sort
of girl to make a great match. I've no
doubt you would make scores of conquests
if you were on the stage, but you're better
off as you are ; if you make your hit, it's
nobody's business to quarrel with you as
to how you do it. I only want to be sure
it's all right, and I'll not stand in your way,
my dear ; I don't want to play marplot on
the occasion.'

' Do one thing for me—keep Miss Tudor
from talking of me, from mentioning my
name at all, in Lady Diana's hearing ;
this is a question of life and death to
me.'

' Dear, dear, I hope not ! there's nothing
so hard to stop as silly people's tongues ;
but I shall see Miss Tudor to-morrow,
before she and my lady meet, and I'll give

her a caution; she'll be afraid to repeat anything in spite of me.'

Vain precaution! on her return home that night, Mrs. Heathcote's face told enough for me to fear there was irreparable mischief done; she met my questions frankly, and said—

'Well, my dear, I've done all I could. I'll tell you everything exactly as it happened, and you shall judge for yourself. Miss Tudor was there before me; she must have gone straight from this house to Lady Diana's, but she never told me a word—very deep of her! There's a sudden intimacy sprung up between those two.'

'I see—Lady Diana chooses one woman as her weapon against another.'

'Not me—she would not try that! but Miss Tudor is a foolish monkey; a titled lady's house is "kingdom come" to her. Well, she was there, but I don't think they had talked much; Sir John was in the room.'

'They did not talk together?'

'Not then. I tried to draw Miss Tudor into a corner, to warn her, but there was nobody but we four, and dinner was announced almost immediately, so I had no opportunity. Sir John was most polite to me : he handed me down to table as if I had been a duchess!' Here Mrs. Heathcote bridled up with pardonable pride; from participation in Miss Tudor's 'little sins,' at least, she was not exempt.

'Wait until you hear exactly what passed. Sir John began to speak of your acting in Desdemona, that time at Stormouth. He praised you very much, and asked me whether I had you with me as a pupil for the stage. It was evident to me you were a common topic of conversation in that house.'

'What did you answer?'

'I said you were with me as a friend. I answered rather stiffly, and gave Miss Tudor a look. I saw through it then, how she and Lady Diana had been plotting together to keep me in the dark.'

'Do you believe that?'

'I am sure of it. Why should Lady Diana never mention your name to me, until Sir John let the cat out of the bag? They've known you were in my house ever since you came, all through Miss Tudor. Sly, deceitful girl!'

'Did she tell them what she heard in church?'

'Every word, my dear, there and then, in spite of my winks, and nudges under the table; she would not see me. She told me afterwards, as we were coming out, that she had no idea what I could possibly mean. I don't believe her.'

'But what did you say to them? Did they question you?'

'Not much; for Lady Diana was taken with a sudden, violent toothache, she said, through the window being open. I don't think that was the reason.'

'A toothache! A heartache! Did she hear his name?'

'Only Arthur. Yes, Miss Tudor told her Arthur. Lady Diana turned very white, and said she was in great pain.'

'I dare say she was; she knows all now.'

I spoke quietly, in a kind of despair. The worst had come, in so far as I was betrayed to my enemy. How far her power to do me harm might reach, I knew not, but from my fears. One thing I was

resolved upon, to tell nothing myself, so
that let what would come, the blame with
Arthur should not be mine. I kept his
behest.

Next morning, at Lady Diana's usual
lesson time, I was in my room, my door
locked, as if I could shut out my fate! I
heard the knock beneath, and the shaking
of the house, as the door closed upon her
within it; a few minutes more, and Mrs.
Heathcote was at my door, knocking and
demanding to be let in. I did not answer
at first; I would not open.

'It is nobody but me,' she persisted;
'let me in, I must speak to you.'

I crept up to the keyhole and groaned
out, 'Keep her off—tell her I'm ill; I can
do nothing, say nothing—go!'

'One minute, for your own sake; I want
to speak to you—let me in.' She was
resolute, and after all, friendly to me.

'Give me your word you will not bring
her in upon me,' I cried : she did so, and I
turned the key in the lock, and fell into her
arms.

'Poor child!' she said, pityingly; 'don't
let that proud, bad woman crush you;

don't be afraid of her, or she will ! Dare her out'; that's your only chance now.'

'She wants to see me—to question me —to put me to torture. The sight of her is enough to kill me. I will wait till he tells me what I must do !'

'I would not put it to that if I were you ; she would only play her game behind your back, and poison his mind, no one knows how. Take my advice, my child ; I would say the same thing to you if you were my own daughter. Face her down, and tell her nothing—that's the way to make her betray herself; she's just the woman to do that.'

'To betray herself ?'

'Yes; she knows that she is a guilty woman. If she has any shame left, she will not dare to push you to extremity, if she sees you will not be trodden on. If you submit or give your own cause up, do not trust to any man to be more true to you than you are to yourself. Take my warning.'

'I will, Heaven help me ! Must I meet her alone ?'

'That is what she wants—but I'll be within call, my dear. Come down.'

I made up my mind to go as it were to
my death, and followed Mrs. Heathcote
down to the drawing-room, where all out-
ward forms of good breeding were to have
place between us three.

'My dear Miss Fortescue, let me present
you to Lady Diana Hope Trevor,' said
Mrs. Heathcote.

My enemy bent her proud head and
smiled an evil smile, while I returned the
honor by a curtsey down to the ground.
Mrs. Heathcote told me afterwards I
looked then the proudest of the two. The
introduction over, she discreetly left us
with, 'I know you two ladies will like a
little chat together. You'll understand
one another better yourselves to yourselves.

Motioning me to sit down, Lady Diana
sank, or rather crouched into an arm-chair,
smooth and subtle as the tigress or the
snake, when meditating the swift spring,
the deadly grasp, the annihilating crush of
a weaker foe.

'I believe we are known to one another
by sight, Miss Fortescue,' she began, with
a cold, cruel ring in her smoothly dropping
words. 'I took an interest in you as Des-

demona, but you were put into a very false position for a young girl.'

'Perhaps so, in the opinion of others ; I did not feel it myself.'

'You suffered very much from nervousness.'

'Not more than others, I fancy. You, Lady Diana, have acted so often, you forget what it is like to stand before the public for the first time.'

'No, indeed, I suffer intensely ; in fact, it makes me quite ill every time I appear.'

'Yet you do it !'

'I am very fond of it.'

'I cannot say I am, or ever could be.'

'And for why ?'

'I have a natural repugnance to drawing the malice of the world upon me !' This I said with an arrow-shot of the eyes at her, but withdrew the glance as it flew. I saw, as well as felt, her eyes dissecting me from head to foot, as if measuring me out to be devoured.

'The malice of the world !' she repeated slowly ; 'yes, that is a fearful thing to any woman who lays herself open to reproach,

but utter ruin to an unprotected girl. I
pity you!'

'Pity me, Lady Diana? That may be
a condescension in one of your rank, to a
mere stranger, but it is not a pleasant compliment. I am content to be what I am,
and not conscious of needing anyone's
pity.' I spoke fast and eagerly, my agitation gaining upon my prudence.   .

'You are very young and innocent—
you *look* very innocent—you have run
away from your home after a man who
does not care for you.'

'I run after a man? Men may run
after me, if they want me.'

'I daresay they may, a good many of
them. You are not handsome, but you
are " fetching " while you are very young,
" *la beauté du diable ;* " though there is not
much of you.' A look of contempt. 'Men
have strange fancies sometimes. You expect to be married to Arthur?'

'I have no right to answer any such
questions; you know nothing about me,
Lady Diana, nor what I expect.'

'Ah, you do? Well, you're a little fool,
that's all ; he is only laughing at you.'

I rose to my feet in the offended dignity of five-feet-four; I was not little, though slight and girlish in figure, and not to be compared with Lady Diana's inches and superb development of womanhood.

'I will not be called a fool,' I said, 'because you, Lady Diana, suspect me of having attracted the regard of somebody you want to keep to yourself; as to laughing at me, that anyone can do at another —you may, if you like, to my face; it will make no difference in what I do.'

She took me at my word, and let go the mocking laughter she had hitherto half restrained; then broke out, 'His wife? pah! He wants you for a mistress; you his wife! ha! ha!'

'Lady Diana, you are slandering a man as incapable of harbouring such a base design as I am of consenting to it.'

'Ah, you love him—he tells you he loves you?'

'You have no right to ask such a question.'

'No right?'

'No. What is it to you what I do? What he does? You are married! Why

should you be jealous of him ?   Why interfere at all ?'

'Jealous! What do you dare to suppose ?   My husband's interests and
Arthur's are bound up together.   He
must not marry out of his class; he must
have connection and influence with his wife,
or remain as he is until his career in India
is secured.   I tell you his prospects will
not suffer him to think of a mere nobody
like you.'

'You take a deep interest in his prospects, Lady Diana.   You will not allow him
to have a wife at all if you can, unless your
husband dies.   Lady Diana, you love him.'

I had hit hard and true upon the mark.
It broke to shivers, which she dashed
away.

'Love him !' she cried ; 'and if I do, so
much the worse for you, if you dare to
come between us ; a chit of a girl that
nobody knows.   Yes ; do whatever you
like, whatever you can.   You are fond of
knocking your head against stone walls.
Ha ! ha !   If the pot of clay will pit itself
against the pot of brass, so much the worse
for the pot of clay.'

Another insolent laugh, to which I had nothing to reply, though the thought of my descent, eight centuries old, made my young blood burn to listen in silence. Boastfully she pursued, trampling on me when she had me down.

'I am of his own caste, his own sphere. I have done for him what no other in England could do. My connections, my husband's influence, my own place in the world, have all been put in motion to the utmost to raise him to his high position ; greatness he had in himself, but the opportunity that made him a great man came through me. He owes me what to him is far more than life—his name, his fame.'

'And how would you have him repay the obligation ? You love him to do him evil, to make him do wrong.'

'Wrong ? There must be wrong, you think. Cannot a woman love a man without disgracing herself ? You judge of others by your own foul thoughts, young lady.'

I felt the hot stream rush scarlet to my face. Here was I, innocent, blurred by contact with my guilty accuser.

'You redden,' she pursued; 'you can blush, it seems. Aye, well you may. No; I am not Arthur's mistress'—a most keenly insulting emphasis on the two words—' not but what many noble-hearted women have given up all, name and rank, and what the world calls honor, for the man they love. A married woman is disinterested—at least, she has all the world to lose for her love, nothing to gain. If she does forsake all for a man, she is better than you girls who sell yourselves to the best bidder in the legal and honorable marriage market, forsooth. Faugh! that is viler than picking oakum or breaking stones. What do you expect your face will fetch? eh, little girl ?—a peerage? Is that the game you want to play ?'

I could endure no more; a lucky thought flashes upon me :

'Say what you will of me, I have done nothing that truth and honor forbid, but you—you have set a taint upon Arthur's finger, a ring of your's that none but himself must wear; you would have him keep it, reckoning on your husband's death, to claim him then—to make him marry you.

You have a husband, and you pledge
yourself to another man. Do you call
this right, or wrong? do you call it honorable?'

'Who told you this?—he has betrayed
me?'

'No; he has kept the wretched secret;
it was not he that told me.'

'Who then?'

'My own eyes—yourself betraying yourself, as women who are capable of these
things will do.'

'Women! What do you know of women
or men either? What do you suppose you
can ever be to Arthur? A stop-gap, a
bagatelle pour passer le temps until old Sir
John sees fit to take himself out of the
way.'

I hardly understood the hideous inuendo;
but fain to guard my own fair fame without
committing him, I said:

'I am no candidate for any conquest, in
any way but what is honorable; I do not
believe any man could doubt that, or
would treat me otherwise.'

'Oh, you believe yourself a paragon of
virtue! You would not be Arthur's

mistress, not you!—except you were a legalised mistress, and so you would be as his wife. You don't expect he could love *you*, if you imagine he loves *me*. What a comparison! His wife, indeed! Men don't marry for a fit of passion!'

Though I shrunk at the horrible revelation, some grain of abhorred truth seemed to thrust itself through her words; had he not left me, undefended, to meet this fury? Was this like loving me as I loved him? Had he not always spoken of her with provoking forbearance, whatever cause brought up her name between us? It was plain he knew she loved him, and he was too tender of her feelings for me to assure myself *that* love could be utterly despised! Was I not indeed a fool? a hopeless one? It might be so, yet if it were possible, I would keep him from her, my abhorred rival!

'Whatever I may be,' 'I said, slowly, 'you can be nothing to him more than a friend—if you call yourself so, you cannot be his wife; though you play dog in the manger all his life long, that gives you no claim upon him.'

'No claim upon him? I, who have raised him to what he is?'

I grew sarcastic: 'Then you ought to be glad of anything that could make him happy; you are married yourself. If he were to marry, you would be on equal terms, that's all; you could wait till his wife died, you know, instead of making him wait for your husband's death.'

'Oh, you cunning young viper! you think to take him from me!—from me, whom he loved all his life, since I was a girl. I might have had him then, if I would: I might have him, if I would do such a thing, now; the man could not resist *me !*'

There was a horrible conviction in her words; should I have driven her desperate had I known her power upon him? She went on—

'No man, once in love with me, ever got over it yet; no more can he. Yes, yes, I can keep him. You think I will stick at anything, having gone so far? That I will be thwarted by a child?—oh no, no!—or a man? Ha! ha! ha! A woman like me will pierce through stone walls if they stand between her and her will. Weak things men are to contend with that! Their fancies, indeed! I can laugh at them, ha! ha! ha!'

She was working herself into hysterical violence, under her simulated defiance of me. I felt, I hoped her power to keep him to a dishonorable tie was less than she assumed; it might be that the demon in her heart should be baffled by my strong and innocent love: I would deal cautiously with her.

'I have no right to answer for Arthur in any way. You have known him long: draw your own conclusions, as you have done hitherto. I have told you nothing.'

'Silence and discretion with a vengeance. I know what you mean to do—to steal a match with him. Not while I live. I will stop that. I will expose him to the world. I will ruin him, utterly—blast his career with infamy. My husband shall be his enemy and my avenger. I care not what I do to myself, if I cut my own throat. Cross me at your peril, young girl; you shall never marry him till you kill me! We'll see which is the strongest, you or I. Ha! ha! ha!'

I thought she was going mad, but she reined in her frenzy fit, and flung herself out of the room. Lost in terror, I had no sense left to conjecture what form her rage might take to destroy me, to do that which I feared above all that could happen to me here or hereafter, separate me from him I loved. I was sitting still, not attempting to stir of my own motion, but trembling with a violent, involuntary seizure in every limb, that shook me like winnowing wheat, when Mrs. Heathcote came and found me.

'My child, what have you done to Lady Diana? She will murder you if she can, or blast you before the world; that is the way that great ladies commit murder of the reputation. I tremble for you.'

I fell upon her breast: 'Oh, women are like devils to other women when they hate.'

'Yes, that's like what Shakespeare says; he was a man. I say men are our worst enemies if we give them their way.'

'Who would have thought it of her, with her soft, blonde beauty? I never knew there could be so much fury in blue eyes.'

'They are the fiercest when provoked. Beware of her! I'm afraid you have been very imprudent. What have you done to her? Oh, I know! You are not to answer any questions. Come upstairs, and write to him, my dear : you shall do whatever you like ; only I have got nothing to say to you. I wash my hands ; you never took me into your confidence.'

'I wish to heaven I could ;' and I sank into her arms weeping. Was she not in place of a mother to me? To something in my misery I must cling, as in the sinking ship, or the burning house, when there is none to help, they cling to one another who are about to perish.

CHAPTER XIII.

MAN PROPOSES.

Not with impunity to me, it seemed, had
Arthur wandered into the paths of virtue
for my sake; his backsliding once discovered by this terrible married woman,
she would contend for him with his honorable love, as devil with angel, striving to
degrade and destroy him body and soul.
He being absent, I could no nothing to
defeat her purpose but write to him in the
way of warning. My great and intolerable
fear was, that on his return she would see
him first, and prejudice my cause. I
wrote :

'You must know at once from myself
that our secret has been suspected, if not

discovered, in the quarter where conceal-
ment was most desired by you; that
misfortune has occurred through no fault
of mine, so come to me and consult how we
must shape our course in the first place, as
soon as you can come back to town ; decide
whatever you wish, but do not be angry
with me—I could not bear it now.

> 'Your ever devoted,
>> 'LEILA.'

When I wrote, I knew he would not be
back for several days, unless my letter were
forwarded ; I was doubtful about that, and
nervous lest it might fall into wrong hands ;
his public character, I knew, brought
bushels of letters through the post, besides
his private correspondence.   I asked Mrs.
Heathcote to send this by a messenger,
with special request that it should be
forwarded.   She did so, half vexed at my
anxiety, then lectured me :

'My child, you are going the way to
lose him ; use him ill, and you will have
a better chance.   Why, I've made my
husband confess, the worse we use a man
the better he thinks of us—before marriage,

I mean. I wish you could marry some one else—a young man, nearer your own age; that would be the way to serve him out.'

'No; I should behave ill myself to do that.'

'Behave ill to a man? And if you did, no matter what we do to men, we may always be sure they deserve it thoroughly on some other woman's account, if not on our own; we can't do anything too bad to them; mark my words—they may yet be useful to you.'

'I thought him the noblest of men—I think so still. Is there no truth, no trust among them?'

'I don't say that altogether, either; he is too old and artful for you, my dear; some young man that had his bread to earn would make you a much better husband; hard work is the only thing that keeps men out of mischief.'

'Your husband—you can trust him?'

'Yes, my dear; we were both very young when we married, and both poor, and we've worked hard together. I will say that for the men in this profession,

compared with men of the world, they are
not so bad.   I can judge ; I've seen a deal
of both : it is the greed of money, or the
care of what the world will say, that spoils
the matches.   A girl had best look on her
admirers as so many fishes that will prey
upon us, unless we prey upon them ; we
have a right to do it—we are the more
generous foe of the two.'

One day all this worldly wisdom might
serve ; it was useless now.

After three days of wretchedness and
suspense, Arthur came, late in the evening,
when it was dark.   Did he fear being
seen ? As I dreaded, it had come to pass ;
she had seen him before me, and fore-
stalled my tale.   His tone was one of the
deepest disappointment—bitter vexation
with himself, half reproach to me.

' How could she know ?' he complained,
' she may have had a suspicion through
some tittle-tattling fool ; she could not
have been certain.   Why, Leila, did you
talk of our marriage ?'

' I did not.'

' Why did you talk to her ? why see her
at all ?'

'She insisted; Mrs. Heathcote put it upon me not to refuse.'

'Mrs. Heathcote? Why did you tell her?'

'I told her nothing; I obeyed you, Arthur. Had I been allowed to take Mrs. Heathcote into our confidence, all this might have been prevented; but it is not my fault, punish me as you will for my misfortune.'

'How could I punish you? how could I bear you to suffer? You are not to blame in any case, but for loving me too well.'

'Am I to blame for that? Oh, don't tell me so; it is too late—I cannot unlove you now!'

'Well, it cannot be helped; it was a great misfortune for both we ever met at all.'

'Oh, don't say that! I cannot bear to think I have caused misfortune to you.'

'Yes; I think worse of it for your sake. What is to be done for you? We cannot marry now; she would ruin my reputation, blast all my career; she told me so, —she means to do it—she has the power.'

'The power to ruin you?'

'Unhappily she has, and some cause to use it, as women reason. Leila, I loved her once; and women hate to yield their power upon a man to another woman.'

'Oh, Arthur! you never told me this before.'

'So much the worse for me now: I should have told you. We loved each other as boy and girl.'

'Your first love?—oh, Arthur!'

'I suppose so. Do not give me those agonising looks, Leila. I never loved her as I have loved you.'

'As you have loved me? Then it is all over now?' And I turned away from him, weeping very sore.

'Do not despair, Leila; but we must be patient. I will tell you the whole truth from the first; you must know it now, and I will make it as gentle to you as I can.'

'Oh, it is all very dreadful to me, and so strange! I thought you above such things; but tell me—you met her long ago?'

'Before you were born, Leila. You have heard I was the architect of my own fame and rank. I was the younger son of a younger son, and went out to India, like Wellington in his day, and many others, to build up our Indian Empire and my own fortunes at the same time. I was then a subaltern in the army, having the *entrée* as a young officer of family, into the highest circles. I met Lady Diana as my superior in the social scale; she was the Viceroy's daughter.'

'You became intimate with her?'

'Well, no; I first saw her at a great ball at her father's palace: I had the presumption to walk up to her and ask her to dance without an introduction.'

'Just like you, Arthur.'

'I was a daring young fellow. Some brother officers were talking about her, and one of them made a wager that I should get snubbed for my impertinence. I forget how it all came about. I went in and won.'

'She danced with you more than once that night?'

'She did, until we were remarked and separated.'

'She was very, very beautiful?'

'The most beautiful, the most fascinating, altogether the most attractive girl I ever met in all my life—she was then.'

'Oh, Arthur! you never could truly love anyone else. You did love her?'

'I thought so at the time, but it came to nothing. I never proposed to her—a man does not, when he has no chance, unless he is a fool.'

'Unless he is in love; then a man can always find a way to do it. She did not encourage you?'

'Yes, she did; her preference for me could not be mistaken; but we never met except in public, when she was surrounded by hosts of admirers. She evidently cared for none of them, yet she treated all too much alike through love of admiration. She never seemed to draw me nearer to her than the others, though I knew she did like me best, and I was too proud to thrust my attentions upon her when I knew it would be no use.'

'Then you did not truly love her. How could you know she would not have you unless you tried?'

'In our relative positions it was impossible I could present myself to her father as a suitor; and I should have thought it dishonorable to tempt her to a runaway match. I had no means to keep her in her station, and she was not a woman to endure poverty.'

'You would not wait until you rose in the army, and then try your chance with her?'

'If I would, she did not; she married, in her own sphere, a man her father's equal in age as well as the rest: that was the worst of the bargain.'

'She did not care for him long?'

'She never cared for him at all—it was a mistake; he was too old for her, and she pined for a lover of her own years, as was but natural.'

'That was unfortunate. General Hope Trevor is a man to deserve a better wife. To me it would make no difference that I was younger than the one I loved.'

'She was unlike you in that, Leila : you loved me for my fame.'

'I did at first—but now for yourself only.'

'Not for my face, Leila?'

'Well, yes—no—I cannot tell for what ; but if you were to turn as black as Othello, it would make no change in me.'

'I believe it, Leila : but she fancied me when I was young, and—well, I had the name of a handsome fellow, the next best thing to being it, and she never fancied Sir John, though she married him with her own free will.'

'You met her after her marriage?'

'Very often, and on much more intimate terms than before.'

'But that was wrong, very wrong of you, Arthur.'

'Why so, when she sought my society? Nothing had ever passed between us that we could not be friends, and no more.'

'Did her husband know?'

'There was nothing to know. He grew very friendly with me, and to his influence, joined with her father's, I owed my rapid advancement to a post which enabled me to fight my way up to the position I have achieved; I believe her family knew of her inclination for me, and felt indebted to my reserve on the occasion.'

'Did they approve of your intimacy with her as a married woman?'

'Oh! they never interfered : Sir John was clever enough and old enough to look after his own wife, I suppose. Perhaps they persuaded themselves they had made all safe when the knot was tied ; we were both too honorable to be suspected.' A slight sarcasm tainted his deep voice with gall as he spoke these last words.

'You saw her very often after her marriage ?'

'Yes ; society was indispensable to her, she said ; and, situated as she was during her husband's frequent absence, she was often deprived of any other congenial companionship, and when left much to herself she became a prey to loneliness, *ennui*, and a morbid longing for a more stirring existence. She suffered from the unwholesome Indian life, with its long intervals of monotony, when a woman, waited upon by a swarm of attendants, has literally nothing at all to do, and the dull current is seldom broken, except by short hot fits of gaiety run mad. Then you have a couple of great balls, or so, and relapse into ditchwater calm again ; I mean the women, of course ; we men had no such humdrum time of it, with the Sikhs and Afghans to manage.'

'Do not English ladies ride through the country?'

'Yes; that is the only change they have. Lady Diana used to ride, she said, until she grew sick of going out alone—that is, with servants only; so I rode with her whenever I was stationed near at hand.'

'You used to act together sometimes?'

'Sometimes; not often. It was a kind of wild excitement with her, and became too painful to both at last. She took to acting with passion, but without judgment, which is one way of making a fool of one's self; it was just a substitute for anything else to do or to think about, a vent for uncontrollable emotions. She can command herself better now than she could then; I could not keep it up at that time as she wished—in fact, I ceased playing at all, as my responsibilities increased. Had I not had this much firmness, we might have been led into what we should have been sorry for.'

'When she could have married you she threw away your love, like a heartless coquette; when she was married herself, she was without excuse to lead you wrong.'

'You are hard upon her, Leila ; believe me, I would rather my tongue and right hand were cut off than I should say there was wrong between us.'

'She kept you from forming any honorable tie, she looked for her husband's death for your sake.   You call this right ?'

'I do not ; but, like most husbands in his position, Sir John seems disposed to thwart any such hopes as his wife may indulge in contingent on his death ; though an old man, I believe he is likely to live long enough to see us both out—me, at least—I am not one of those iron constitutions.'

'She has spoiled all your life—you will never love another so well——'

'I gave proof to the contrary, Leila, in seeking you ; I was weary of my hard bachelor's life, when your affection came to me like an angel's visit, and I longed to attach to my side so sweet a companion ; I hesitated, I own, in view of the obstacle, but by thinking and thinking my plans were laid—first of all to make you my own

by a secret union, then, on my return to
India next autumn, I intended you should
come out under the protection of a lady
and her husband, friends of mine, and live
with them, not known to be my wife, but
often together—very often.'

'You would have made me your Amy
Robsart—poor Amy! she had a cruel end
—but I should have consented to a like
death to have known her happiness.'

'God forbid, Leila! I have enough to
answer for already; you would have been
content to return to your native land of the
sun, to live in silence and secret, as in a
dream, with me to give you every hour
that I could spare from ruling its destinies?
You would have been happy as my wife, to
lose all the world besides?'

'Oh, too, too happy! You could do
this?'

'I told no one—but my friends would
not refuse to protect you; until we were
married safe, I did not dare to trust our
secret to them; it seems my caution was
needed—too sorely needed!'

'I suppose, then, it was not to be! I
ought not to have consented. Had I

been your wife, with any doubt about me, what would my father say to me, if he lived?'

'True, true! You had no right to run any risk, because you were an unfriended orphan; I should not have asked that of you I could not have expected of another; but I meant all well, all in honor. I trusted to achieve so secure an eminence, that in time I should overcome any mortal's power to injure me or mine; ultimately, I hoped to lead you through the world at my side.'

'You say so to me as if you knew it could never, never be.'

'I cannot tell at present; I would not draw upon myself, I dare not draw upon you, the revenge of a woman in her desperation.'

'What is it that she can do?'

'I know not what she can *not* do—she has the will. If I outraged her feelings openly by marrying you, she can expose all that has passed between her and me, and in that case, the worst construction is what the world always puts upon every indiscretion; her husband, now my fast friend, would become my deadly enemy; she would do that, if she were to blast herself along with me. This would involve my fall from place, power, fame, all I have won so hardly, and make my name a title of execration—just the same as happened to Byron in his time; the people of England have their indignation fits to punish such high placed offenders.'

'Lady Diana would bring this upon you —and herself?'

'She would do anything. If there be no other way to conquer me, she will fight me with fire, like the princess in the Eastern story, who fought the enchanter with his own weapons, until both perished in the flames—but she was conqueror. The woman always is who will sacrifice herself to destroy her foe.'

'But, Arthur, she cannot divide us for ever without your will—with my will she shall not.'

'Judge me out of your own heart, Leila; you love me too well to desire my ruin, involving too, yourself; no other result could follow, were we to marry now.'

'Not now; but even if never to marry, I could be content, happy, more than happy, if I felt sure you loved me.'

'That, Leila, you wrong us both to doubt, after all that has passed between us.'

'But must we be parted, whose hearts God has joined together by circumstances so wonderful, so strange? Must a false, bad woman have the power——?'

'Hush, Leila! have some respect for one of your own sex, who has suffered as I trust you never can suffer.'

'Don't say that; you know not what I am capable of for your sake.'

'A passionate, utterly disappointed woman, who for her worst misfortune has herself to blame—there is no sting like that to embitter failure.'

'I am to blame that ever I gave myself to you heart and soul. Oh, do not throw back the fatal gift now! If not as your wife, let me cling to you as your devoted friend —like a child to a father—like a dog to one who has shown it kindness—at least let me see you sometimes, let me not be thrust away from you—not far away, and you gone to the other ends of the earth.

Let me follow—if not your wife, I am—I am—your love.'

He knew I spoke in innocence, like Elaine, thinking no harm ; he smiled tenderly, sadly, but with a firm voice made answer, ' That cannot be.'

' Then there is nothing more to be said, but I must die.'

' Die, Leila ?'

' It is better for me to die than to live, deserted and miserable. It is more than I can bear ; I long to die !'

' That is madness, Leila ; you, so young, so brilliantly gifted. Leave misery to those who have deserved their own misfortunes ; the world is before you yet.'

' The world is nothing to me ; I have no father, no mother, no friend but my poor old grandmother, who, if I were to die tomorrow, would shed a tear for me. Oh, God, I wish I could ! You—you were all my world, and I have lost you, Arthur !

' Don't say that, my own Leila ; with time and patience we may overcome all things.'

'But you will not let me go with you to India?'

'No, darling; you must return home; you are better disposed there, until I can honorably claim you; until then the less we meet the better. If you could bear to meet day after day, as we have met these weeks past, and be no more than that to each other—if you could bear it as an innocent girl, I as a man could not; it is best that we should be parted; God knows that in all that has passed between us you have had enough of wrong.'

'But her—you will not meet her? There is a ball at the palace to-night; she will be there; but you—you will not go?'

'Nay, I must; my official position makes it an obligation; but what of that, Leila? Amongst a thousand people, what harm can one woman do to a man?'

'Oh, Arthur, you will meet her there, where I am excluded——'

'In public what can it matter? I am not in a position to shun her society like the plague. Forgive me, Leila; I did not say that to give you pain, unreasonable child.'

14—2

He caught me to his breast in one embrace—one only. Oh, how unlike our parting as it was wont to be! A kiss upon my fore-head, a passionate, despairing kiss, and he left me to my grief alone!

CHAPTER XIV.

WOMAN DISPOSES.

AFTER he was gone I began little by little
to realise, to see clearly through the horrid
situation ; then I knew that his influence
had bound me with a strong spell to submit my will to his. In his presence, it would
seem passion slept ; now the awful fire that
should consume my life's springs, subdued
and satisfied for a moment by sight of him,
sprang up anew to torture me, and could
not be quelled by my effort. Now was
the truth sensible to me : I had misread my
course with him, I had been too tame !

My own will and judgment I must not
so easily give up—if he went to India,
thither I must follow ; I had the right to
breathe the same air, if not to see him,

rather than put half the world between us.
No need of that. We at least were not
divided by a gulf of sin and shame, such
as he must wade through to reach her. I
could go to India and seek a harbour with
my mother's kindred : was I not born
there ? That right of birth should stand
me in stead now, and the bright inheritance
of my dear father's fame, I could not
doubt, was remaining there for me.

The room shook with the rolling of
carriage wheels ; I heard and felt them
night after night since I came to town. We
lived in a nook of a street close by a fashionable neighbourhood. I had not yet grown
accustomed to the perpetual noise, rolling
and rolling continually, as they bore the
gay throngs from scene to scene of fes-
tivity, to banquet and ball, where those
two might meet one another, where he
might meet all the world as it lay at his
feet, and whence I was shut out. Those
wheels rolling and rolling on as if for ever
—they bore upon my brain now !

I called to mind, involuntarily, every
word I had heard said by Mrs. Heathcote
and others, of her, of him. There was no

shutting out the conviction that, whatever
I might believe the truth to be, the world's
condemnation had been passed upon the
liaison, silently, and without scandal, inasmuch as the husband was quiescent ; but if
he were to add his voice, then indeed it
would be the ruin of Arthur's fame and
name. It might be there was no guilt accomplished yet, only the suspicion of it
clinging to him through her. To ward off
such suspicion he might be led—heaven
knows to what. Had not that woman
boasted to me of her power over him as if
she gloried in her very shame ?

Jealousy, yes, horrible jealousy, entered
into my breast like the possession of a
demon. I took measure of her, as she
had done of me, in hate and loathing ;
every detail of her face, form, and manner
of speech became present with me. Now,
even now, was she spreading for him the
snare of her beauty and fascination, with
every allurement of pernicious charm
to betray a man to death and perdition.
I could feel the wondrous texture of her
milk-white arms, round and soft like a
babe's, emerging half seen from their

ruffles of rich lace ; her bosom's rise and
fall I could perceive through the mist of
vaporous gauze—like bright clouds floating before the moon's fair orb, that men's
eyes should the more desire the full lustre
of her loveliness.   My thoughts shaped an
image of her form, grandly moulded, like
the statue of a Roman Empress.   Oh,
me ! I had no beauty to contend with
hers !

It was ten o'clock when my resolution
took shape ; something I saw palpably
before me was leading me on to do it.
The step was a desperate one—to go that
very moment and seek him out, wherever
he might be, to forbid him meeting her
again on the peril of his soul and mine !

Prudence, reputation, consequence, I forgot them all, meaning no ill.   There was
no one to advise or detain, no one to ac-
company me—Mrs. Heathcote and her
husband were both on duty at the theatre.
I reasoned with myself : Arthur was,
perhaps, gone to the ball, and I should be
too late to find him.   No matter, I must
go !

I went ; I reached his abode, chambers

apart from his official residence, where he had given me of late his private address ; a carriage was at the door, I recognised on it the Hope Trevor arms ; was it waiting there for her or her husband ? If the latter, what would he think of me ? I could not stop myself now ; my attempt had passed beyond my own control.

I obtained entrance, and stood upon the first landing, before his door ; there was a demur to my coming in by the servant who opened it ; some one was speaking in the room within. Through a closed inner door beyond I recognised her ; I grew actually bold, that had trembled like a fallen leaf till then. What right had this evil-hearted married woman to come between me and my love ? Oh, how I abhorred the thought ! I would dare her out to the bitter end ! I glided past the servant, and—I know not how—passed through the obstacle of the inner door. I stood before them like the spectre of their own dead conscience : pale as a spasm of remorse, the accusing angel who will keep no silence, I stood there uttering not a word, as I smote him with my eye.

He neither spoke nor moved, but to lay his hand across his brow, as if in sharp pain ; she—she glared at me, like the wild cat from the hollow of a tree, measuring the length between her and her victim's throat, yet doubtful of her own strength to spring so far ; her brow grew black with the wrath pent within her heart, her blue eyes darkened, while she hissed between her teeth, rather than said, 'What brings you here, young lady ?'

I was past all fear, all respect of consequences to myself or others. Arthur looked at me with imploring signs to be silent and to go. It was in vain, he had lost all power upon me now. I answered, as it was borne in upon me to answer, calm and proud, as she was fierce and beside herself with wrath : 'My Lady Diana, I am come for reasons of my own, with which no stranger has the right to take concern ; as to meeting your ladyship in this company, I did not expect the honor, nor certainly should I have aspired to it.'

'Oh, I quite understand ! You came to enjoy the gentleman's society *en tête-à-tête*. My presence is inconvenient, not being a

chaperon of your own choosing, yet I think,
for a young lady of your birth and position, you venture a good deal. Suppose I
were to tell our mutual friends and ac-
quaintances of this pleasant little encounter?
What should you think of that, Miss
Fortescue ?'

'Please yourself, Lady Diana, amongst
your own circle. I am quite sensible I do
not belong to it, neither do I hold myself
answerable for what others may say of me
contrary to truth ; I have done nothing of
which I ought to be ashamed. Can you
say as much ? Suppose that I, or any one,
spoke of you to your husband, as I have a
right to speak ?'

I was carried out of myself so far, and
there I stuck in the slough of shame; I
could not utter the black thought within
me, but she, being guilty, understood me
well, and braced herself to assume the
boldness of the desperately bad among
women.

'What do you dare to hint at ? Take
care what you say, young girl ; remember
your station is beneath me, you have no
right to speak a word of what I choose to

do, nor conjecture about my conduct. Aha !
at your peril provoke a blow between
us.'

'You are not at the Queen's ball to-
night,' I said ; 'you make General Hope
Trevor believe you are there ; your very
dress betrays the game you play.'

She glanced in alarm at the marvellous
pile of azure satin, pink gauze clouds, and
folds of lace, lighted up with a huge wealth
of jewels, all so combined as to make her
beauty a wonder and delight to the eyes of
men. The room felt faint with the rich
scent of many coloured roses blended with
her adornment ; from the cunning intricacies
of her hair, down to the edge of her airy
draperies. She looked at herself and then
at me ; trembling, I know not whether with
rage or fear, she turned upon me :

'I shall be at the Queen's ball, if I
am not there yet. I choose my own time,
and my own movements ; I refuse to have
you set yourself as a spy upon me. You,
sir, call this young person your friend, I
suppose. If you are not my enemy, order
her to quit your house.'

'I will go myself when you go, Lady

Diana, but not before,' I cried ; 'otherwise
I tell your husband.'

She burst into a horrid laugh. 'What
can you tell my husband? you think you
can make him believe your word against
mine and Arthur's? We shall deny every
syllable you can say.'

'He shall hear the truth, whether he
believes it or not: you came here, Lady
Diana, to corrupt and ruin, if you can,
your husband's friend ; are you not ashamed
—I blush for you—a woman to tempt,
seduce a man—it is too horrible.'

'Go, go away—away! I cannot suffer
this. Arthur, am I here to be insulted in
your presence, and you stand by? Turn
her away, turn her away! Rid me of the
sight of her !'

What a face Arthur turned upon me ;
that broke my spirit within my heart! He
forced me out of the room, I know not
how, with a faint promise to see me on
the morrow. 'Oh, Leila,' he whispered,
'you have ruined all ; undone yourself and
me !'

I know no more, shall never know.
I had a dream that night, although I never
closed an eye ; I saw in spirit——

I arose with the morning, yet not I, Leila Fortescue; it was another—a broken thing, a strange, older face that met me in the glass with a look I recognised not as my own; it was as though ten years had gone in that one waking night.

I had thrust myself in where I should not, and he would hate me now. I dressed my hair as usual, mechanically; among its dark depths I found some grey hairs scattered like untimely snow upon the buds in their April bloom.

CHAPTER XV.

LOVE, THOU ART BITTER.

AND Arthur kept his promise, to the letter
that killeth, if not in the life-giving spirit
of hope. That first day of my despair he
came early in the forenoon; his first look
of estrangement was enough—I knew, yes,
I knew.

No question did I ask him; tenderly
and reverently as a father had I ever
thought of him; though the deep tone of
his voice, as it softened to me, and the
magic of his eye, had stirred my heart to
its utmost depths with the thrill of an unknown passion—my first and last. This
was the love that lives through life unto
eternity, passing with the soul within the
gates of death, and rising pure as immortal

light upon the angel's eyes—the virgin veil
that trembled upon my heart enclosed his
too in its tender embrace, until now that
this suffered profanation. I blushed for
him as a part of myself; I burned with
shame at the outrage that another woman
had beguiled his love. Let me doubt, if
possible, rather than believe the worst!
If this were true, let me be deceived!
Had the marriage vows been 'as dicers'
oaths' to them ? or, while the heart lapsed
from virtue, had the feet kept to the narrow
path of honor at least ? Let there remain
a doubt upon it for ever ! I remember
how, when a child, I had heard my grandmother tell the story of Nelson and Lady
Hamilton ; in no measured terms of reprobation did she speak of ' England's darling
hero ' on that theme. I did not understand then, but as I grew up to read
history, the early deep impression led me
to examine for myself the justice or falsehood of the aspersion that blurred one of
England's brightest glories. I found it
recorded in the truthful page, how Nelson
owed to a woman's helping zeal the first
victory that made him great; that the

woman was beautiful exceedingly, and in her unfriended youth had been tempted through that beauty into error ; that she married an honorable man, and, as his wife, met Nelson, her husband's friend, and, as such, served his interests together with England's welfare. I learned how Nelson loved this woman with a grateful love, so honorable in itself that the whole story of their friendship, and how much she had done on his behalf, was written by him to his wife, act by act and word by word—I read how this love grew to a devouring passion, how Nelson yielded up his heart, estranged from his wedded wife, to her whose gift was fame. I marked how suspicions arose, in private, in public, all over the world, yet how the recording pen says, if that great heart wandered, we must deplore the alloy of human weakness in the noblest born of England's worthies— that error led to guilt was doubtful at the worst, so must be left for ever. The chaste virgin muse of history would blush to tell a sadder, more ignoble tale !

And so, as England felt for her Nelson's fame, the like did I for my hero-love.

That he had betrayed his friend's trust to rob him of the honor of his wife—no, anything but that! I could not look in Arthur's face and believe such a thing of him!

It was long—how long I know not—before either of us could find a word to speak to the other, and, when his utterance came at last, how faint it sounded in its inexpressible sadness! 'Leila,' he faltered, in hoarse whispers, 'oh, Leila, we are both undone ; yet spare me and yourself what would do no good to either now.'

'Spare you ?' I cried. 'You have come to me to ask—what? My silence? You have not deserved it from me ; you have trampled on my dearest feelings, and for her, that woman! You remember my dead father! Should his daughter's heart be poorer than a worm's, think you? I was not born to be the abject slave, the plaything of a man !'

'Leila, you are very bitter against me.' I could not be that; I bowed my head and sobbed in agony—he saw his power. 'Leila, if you would have your revenge of me, take it. God knows you have the right, as surely as you have the opportunity;

go, if you will, to that woman's husband, and tell him you found her closeted with me alone last night, when he believed she was at the palace ; repeat to him whatever you overheard.'

'No ; I shall not do that.   I heard nothing but the sound of her voice, and I rushed in—perhaps I had a right—but, Arthur, I am no listener, and if I were, I could not bear to hear——' My voice was choked in my throat by the hard grip of pain.

'Leila, it is in your hands to make the world my enemy ; there is no man's heart but would take your side, who have no father, no protector——'

'Oh, true, true ! You were the safer in betraying me.'

'No ! I tell you, no.   There I am most without excuse, without chance of mercy from those who out of my fault would feed their envy to my ruin.   Set me at issue with Sir John Hope Trevor for that worthless woman's sake, all England looking on at the tragic farce, and this day six months I shall write myself, not Viceroy of India, but knave, impostor, fool, or what my

15—2

enemies' worst malice will.   Be it so, if you are my enemy, Leila ; but for you, and you alone, remember, all this had never been.'

'You mean that I was wrong to love you, Arthur, or if I could not help that, even to dare hope when you bade me hope.   I did not seek you unmaidenly, Arthur ; had you never spoken I could have suffered in silence, I knew you were so far above me !'

'Leila, you would be a wife for a hero or an emperor, if he were but free.   I am not ; that is the poison of the curse upon me !'

'Not free, you say, because of a married woman, your friend's wife ?   Oh, Arthur, it was hard not to tell me at first the bitter truth.   What had I done to you, that you would not spare me this ?   This quenching of the hope you yourself kindled, till it grew to be all my life—you tear it from me, when to part with it I must die.   Why, why did you not save me from this misery ?'

'I thought not to go so far as I did ; I was charmed with you, Leila, fascinated

without knowing it : I did not expect you
to love me to your hurt at my age ; to me
you were a child.'

'Not such a child as to be content with
a half share in your affections, halting between me and a woman I cannot speak of
but with a stain upon my lips ; rather than
that, I will rend my heart in two, and cast
you out of it ; am I child or woman now ?'

'Leila, to your own heart's content you
have power to wring mine ; I have deserved
the worst you can say or do to me, only too
well.   Not to excuse myself, who am without excuse, I tell you I did not reason—I
loved you, when it was only madness to
yield to such passion ; I loved you, as a
man, not naturally prone to evil, loves the
one woman who could bring an earthly
heaven into his arms in her purity and
devoted tenderness. I saw but the rapture
of the end, and seized the readiest means,
roughly, and without reflecting enough
upon the risks to both ; what a man longs
for too much, too ardently, becomes reality
to his hope—though with that hope de-
ferred or crossed another's innocent heart
must sicken as well as his own. I have

deserved that your love should turn to
hate.'

'Yes, if I could hate, loathe you, that
would be something less wretched than
what I suffer now! Oh, Arthur, how you
have humiliated me, broken my pride in
your true nobility of soul; you have de-
faced, as you only could, the image of your
own glory in my heart; you have covered
my love with shame and dishonor in my
eyes !'

I had spoken too much—he could not
bear to hear any more : my words were
sharp daggers, driven home by his own
conscience, whose strength, not mine,
thrust through his heart. Mechanically he
rose to go. I saw it; I sprang forward as
if to stay him with one wild clasp. Shame
held me back. I fell upon the ground at
his feet, for my spirit had well-nigh gone
from me. He rang the bell, called Mrs.
Heathcote; she raised me up, while he bent
over me, but did not touch me; that was
all I knew, and so I was left to my despair.

I believe I took it very quietly, after
reluctant hope had given her last death
throe ; anyhow, I did not go mad yet, and,

being asked by Mrs. Heathcote what I
meant to do—whether I would not return
to my grandmother at home ?—coolly
answered—' By-and-by, after the performance next Monday.'

' My dear, what have you got to do with
that ?' remonstrated Mrs. Heathcote : ' you
don't want to go to Woolwich, surely ?
—you're too ill for this extra fatigue.'

' I am not—I mean to see her act.'

' What! to go in front ? You can't go
alone, and who is to take you ?'

' Are you not going ? Why can't I go
with you ?'

' My dear, 'tis impossible. I shan't be
in front ; I'm going to direct the performance and keep the amateurs together, as
I've got the chance to be out of the bill
here next week. You can't sit and be
stared at alone in a crowd, and before your
friends, too. What would Arthur think of
you ?'

' True : he must not see me there. Are
there no private boxes ?—I would give any
price—no place where I could see and be
hid ?'

' Nothing of the sort ; unless you want

to make a public show of wearing the willow ; that's just the interpretation all the world will put upon your poking your little face among those people, a young girl like you.'

'Then I must not ; but I shall remain here till it is over, and remember, I trust to you for a true account of the whole business.'

'And so you may, my dear ; that's the most sensible thing you can do under the circumstances, unless you would go home at once and drive the whole concern out of your mind.'

'I will do so afterwards. I could not stir from this, in any peace, until next Monday night is over and I know whatever you have to tell me afterwards.'

'All right, my dear ;' and so we settled it. I remained in town until over the Monday, and Mrs. Heathcote's story of that night was mixed up in a grotesque jumble with the preparations for my journey, altogether like the ugly mocks of an impossible dream, less absurd than the derisions of our waking sleep of life.

My first question to Mrs. Heathcote was

about Arthur. Was he behind the scenes during that night ?

' Never saw him at all, good or bad, or in front either.'

' Was he not there ?'

' Of course he was bound to be there, but he was not proud of the position ; he hid himself among the audience somewhere. Sir John came round before we began, and complimented me on my part of the business. Oh, he was quite delighted !'

' Indeed ! I have heard him say he wished Lady Diana would give up acting altogether.'

' Very likely, but his wishes have nothing to do with what she chooses ; and, as Lady Diana must act, it is quite right her husband should feel his obligations to the professionals who help her not to make too great a fool of herself. Oh ! she'll act as long as she can stand. Sir John is a brave, dear old duck—any woman could turn him round her little finger. If I were a young lady to be married, I would choose him for my husband '

' Did she please herself, and her audience ?'

'Not worse than usual. All the men
on leave in her husband's old regiment had
free tickets for the gallery, and, of course,
they would applaud the general's wife;
that's her idea of a "great success." Well,
there are women on the stage just as
bad.'

'As bad actresses? or as unfair in the
way of applause?'

'Both one and the other. Lady Diana
has talent—decided talent. If she had
gone on the stage at sixteen, and worked
her way up, she might have made a great
actress; as it is, I consider she does me
more credit than any pupil I have had for
so short a time. I should like to teach
her for twelve months. I never knew she
had so much stuff in her. Mrs. Cibber
has been spoiling her, and has taken such
a lot of money for it. Well, I never say
anything against another professional. I
should have taught her to walk first.'

'Taught her to walk?'

'Yes, to walk, not shambling along as if
her knees were tied together under her
train, and twitching it every now and then
out of her way. An actress has no busi-

ness to touch her train, or to know that she has one. 'Tis odd how ladies who go to court can be so awkward with their trains on the stage. She could not even carry her dress, I don't know how she could dance in it. One of the officers told me he saw it on her at the Queen's ball.'

'The ball at the palace last week? Then she did go after I saw her in his own room with Ar——?' I caught myself on the slip of the tongue, and was struck silent; so, for some moments, was Mrs. Heathcote, but after a long stare at me she got out—

'Oh! ah!' then, after another pause filled up in the same way, 'I thought that gentleman had something to do with your nocturnal expedition. You saw her with him? at his chambers, you mean? and she went to the ball afterwards, of course; people do strange things sometimes, but a young girl like you at a man's chambers! The very last place she ought to have seen you in. I don't wonder she made her account of you there.'

'What business had she—— ?'

'You've got nothing to do with that;

she would know where to stop, how to save appearances ; besides, she's safe as a married woman, whatever she chooses to do. So long as her husband's eyes are shut it's nobody's business to interfere.'

'What ! then you think he would put up with—— ?'

'Anything at all, he would, I declare I believe, and think no harm of his wife. Oh, he's a noble old fellow ! I hope he's not deceived in her ; she did go lengths with the young fellow who played De Neuville, the lover—it was Mrs. Cibber's business, she said at rehearsal : Mrs. Cibber, indeed ! Whatever she makes her pupils do is sure to be disgusting ; why, Lady Diana kissed the man three times— not stage kisses either. Business is business, but when amateurs can't draw the line, they run into downright impropriety.'

'She had a motive, perhaps, to make some one jealous—not her husband.'

'I know what you mean. I think De Neuville took it she was smitten with his charms in earnest. Any vain young fellow would ; she drove him mad over his part. He got up in the night to rehearse, and

walked up and down his room repeating
his words in his night attire.   Mr. Heathcote could not sleep in the room beneath him.
She has a great deal to answer for there ;
if she only did it to make someone else
jealous, she went very far with him.'

'Did the public—did her friends like
it ?'

'Her friends, as you say, not the public.
She would have been hissed for such in-
decorum if she were an actress on the stage.
Her friends enjoyed it.   I heard a titter in
the stalls, and they did laugh at her exit
up the steps ; she would have six steps,
and the lime light, if you please, to throw
out her diamonds and make up—she
would have anything that cost more
money.   Well, as she got up the steps
her train rolled down them, like a jack in
the box coming out, and set the audience
in a roar : it was irresistible.'

'That must have put her out very much,
what with the excitement she had before ?'

'Not a bit worse than every time she
acts ; she always manages to keep some
hold on her senses, like a half madwoman
out on leave.'

'She does not forget what she has to say?'

'Oh, no! she speaks her words all right, but she can't walk, and Mrs. Cibber can't teach her——'

'Perhaps Mrs. Cibber did not try?'

'Perhaps not; I should, if she were twenty years younger, but she's too old to be taught, that's about the end of it when all's said and done.'

Cruel Mrs. Heathcote, how I loved you!

CHAPTER XVI.

SWEET IS DEATH TO ME.

READER, have you ever noted, in the official death returns, how many suicides every year occur amongst the young? How many in the opening flower of their age, seventeen and eighteen, ay, fifteen and sixteen, find the burthen of life so intolerable at its dawn, as by their own act to cut it off rather than strive to reach its noon hours of rest, that pause on the path of weary labour, the reward of patient endurance in strife which conquers all mortal obstacles, and melts the obduracy of fate itself? These children of sorrow know not by experience of the effect of Time's slow but sure healing hand. Their first affection, their first trust deceived, the one blow leaves them with the broken spirit that mortals may not bear and live : it seems to them as if there were nothing left worth living for, no cause to renew the struggle beyond their strength to suffer, being not accustomed to the world's misery. Thus, after one fatal mistake, will rash, bright youth fling away its future—so easy is it then to die—much to the wonder of the old, who cling with such tenacity to the poor remnant of mere existence, with no pleasure in it left, when the last flicker of life-fire is just dipping beneath the brink of the open grave.

It seemed as though I too were about to die. I came home changed in manner and in face; the health and elastic spring of youth had gone away from me; my industry and cheerful ways all lost. My step was heavy and languid, as if my weight were more than my feet could bear, though my slight, girlish form had lost all roundness, and the slender bones were peering through the wasted flesh on neck and fingers. I was a spectacle and a marvel to the keen observation of our little world, a provoking object to my grandmother's surprise and angry pity.

'What can be the matter with the girl?' she puzzled herself to discover one day, having been irritated by the remarks of Mrs. Nightingale, the jealous, as to my extraordinary 'going off' in bloom and spirit, and dark hints as to the possible causes, various complaints being first enumerated as incident to young girls; finally, dissatisfaction at being still without a husband was hit upon as a reasonable excuse for my 'wasting away as thin as a whipping-post;' and for this mischance, both Mrs. Nightingale and my grandmother agreed, with some inconsistency, I was myself chiefly in fault, having shown the disposition of a little coquette, by whom men dislike being made fools of. But, Grannie added, I was quite a child, and she hoped would know better next time, and not throw away a woman's only chance of any happiness in the world.

'What is wrong with you, my child?' she asked in kindness, when we were alone together; 'do you wish to marry, now that you have put it out of your power to make a conquest, as you ought to have done? I'm afraid we must be content with a humbler match now.'

'No, Grannie, I will never marry beneath me.'

'I do not wish that you should ; you are not fit to marry anyone but a gentleman of good birth, but we can never expect such another match as George Mauleverer. I knew at the time you would be sorry. I told you when you were doing it there would come a time when you would give the whole world, if you had it, to undo the fatal mistake of throwing such an offer away. Is that what you are feeling now ? Oh ! how well I knew you would ; how I prayed, and lowered myself more than I ought, to sue to you for pity for your own sake, and I might as well have reasoned with a stone wall, or an iron gate ; and now, when it can't be helped, you have no patience to bear what you brought upon yourself and me with your eyes open.'

'Grannie, you are mistaken—I am not fretting after George Mauleverer ; if he were free to renew his offer now, I should refuse him again. I am glad he's married.'

'Then you ought not to say that to me. How can you expect ever to do any good, when you fly in the face of a parent ? You

ought to have been married to him ; it is
very bad for me you were not—I should
have had peace then.'

'I could not love him—I never could.'

'Pah ! I've no patience with such stuff.
What's the matter with you, then ?   You're
killing yourself with grief ; ruining your
looks, and spoiling your voice, the only
two things that a woman can advance herself in the world by.   Is it for a man you
are doing it ?   Oh Lord ! there's nothing
so dreadful as girls in love to anyone who
has the care of them !   Oh, what an unfortunate old woman I am !   But surely if
you were in love, at least you would tell it
all to me ! That's impossible.'

So much the better that she concluded
so.   She was the last to whom I could
bear to tell such a thing.   Between her
world and mine lay the gap of a generation ;
she could not be to me as a fond mother,
to pour my grief into her bosom and be
comforted, to bear life for her sake who
gave it.   I had frustrated her desire to
force happiness upon me after her own
views of woman's chief good, and she
could have no patience with my reasonless,

causeless sorrow, which she took as an offence and reproach to her own bringing up of me. Struck with another idea through my silence, she exclaimed, of a sudden :

'Is this a passion for the stage? If so, Lily, I had rather consent and let you try to do the best you could than see you die. Perhaps you would not be allowed to act— you ought to tell me what happened to you in London, and I could give you my advice.'

'You are wrong there, Grannie—I have no wish for the stage—I had rather you left me to myself; there is nothing the matter with me, indeed.'

'Nothing the matter with you! and you shedding tears from morning till night? That would be a bad tale to be told of me —I will not live in the house with you—I shall lose my character through you, as well as the rest: you have ruined my peace of mind and broken my heart already, that's all the thanks I have got—no mother ever sacrificed herself to a daughter as I have done to you, and to be made feel " how sharper than the serpent's tooth is

an ungrateful child,"' and, with this mis-
quotation against me, she rushed out of the
room.

I went to bed, where I could weep my
fill unquestioned, and take my miserable
pleasure in hot tears.   I knew there would
come hours when I should refrain, when
all the water in my eyes should be shed,
and they needs must dry up in their
sockets, until nature should replenish their
fountains : I dreaded the dark, and left my
candle lighted upon the foot of my bed—
I did not expect there was any sleep for
me.   I lay awake several hours, but at
last fell asleep, the candle still burning : it
must have burned on till it came down to
the paper in the socket of the candlestick,
and after lighting that, the flame communi-
cated itself somehow to the bed-clothes and
mattress, not to burn up conspicuously, but
with a dull smouldering, such as a breath
would blow into a blaze, and set the house
on fire : as it was, the room was filled with
smoke when I awoke out of a dream of
strangling and suffocation to see the red
edges of fire creeping like worms in the
dark through the coverings of my bed—

another moment and I must have been stifled. I found my way to the window and flung it wide open ; then a flame rose, but I flung a jug of water upon it, dragged the bed-clothes over, and crushed it down into darkness : then I could not see, nor find my way out of the room, and the thick smoke was struggling with my breath. Though the door was shut, it filled the house with the smell of burning. My grandmother was aroused by it, and rushed about in her long night-dress, thinking the house was burning down ; she came into my room, with a lighted candle in her hand, to look for the fire. I told her I had just put it out, which she did not believe till she had searched every corner and cupboard and found no fire, but the remains of my burnt bed-clothes, and some marks of fire on my night-dress : then I told her how narrowly I had escaped being burnt to death, and how thankful I felt there was so little mischief done.

This was not her view of the adventure.

' Nearly burnt in your bed ! Is that the tale you have to tell me ? O Lord, what a disgrace ! If I had not been here to watch

you, the house would have been burnt
down, I suppose. Oh Lord! and the
servants will see you've burned all the bed.
I'm well punished for your not being married. Oh Lord! Oh Lord! What a curse
it is to have such a child!'

' I am sorry to be alive to trouble you.
I might have died for want of air, without
the house being burned, if I had waked a
few moments later. I am sorry it was not
so, since you take my escape of death as
you do.'

'Oh, Lily! Lily! you are killing me!
How can you say such a thing to me? My
character will be taken away from me,
along with the rest, if I live with you
any longer—there must be a separation—
there is no other way to have any peace
with you.'

I took her at her word, as if she meant
what she said. I would not keep a hateful
life by eating her bread any more. I knew
not what I should do—I put on my hat
and shawl and went out, wandering away
alone by the sea shore, with no fixed intent
but one—never again to return to my
home; my grandmother would think better

of me if I were dead—we should vex each
other no longer.

Through the death of mortal love, as
through the death of mortal life, the bruised
spirit is fain to pass, under the hand of
God, alone ; we are like the wounded bird,
or the fawn with an arrow in her side, on
broken wings or nerveless feet, dragging
itself out of sight of its former companions,
ready to shun it in its misery, laying itself
down, amid some hidden covert beneath
the leaves to perish in secret.

Not seventeen, and longing to die !
Yes ; the strong and terrible desire of death
was upon me now, and seemed to draw me
back into the earth, from whence the fair
beauty of all things springs—as Cyrus, the
great king, when dying, told his sons, and
bade them bury his royal corse in the
universal grave. I looked upon the grace
of my young form that I wished to destroy,
and let the dust return to the earth as it
was ; it pitied me for that, until I matched
in imagination my pale girlish charms
against her radiant beauty. What were
all my poor attractions beside that Lamia's
dazzling wealth of them to reduce a hero

to her will?—hers, that evil-hearted, terrible
woman who had corrupted the noble
nature to which all my being clung. Are
stolen waters so sweet to man? would she
entice him to set at nought her marriage
vows, the only oaths a man may violate
without infamy? I never believed she
could. While I was near him, I could not
lift my eyes upon his face to think foul
shame of him ; but now that she had parted
us, a hideous light was forcing itself into
my eyes, and turning my love for Arthur
into heart-hate and disgust, more bitter far
than the sting of my own humiliation. I
knew that he would never write to me
again, after I left London, nor did he ; I
had nothing except two or three letters of
his, and a camellia, faded but tenderly
preserved—his gift in exchange for my
living heart. I drew it from my bosom,
where I kept it, and the cold earth felt
gentle to me as the sweet bosom of the
mother that bore me, her only child ; the
evening fell upon me as I lay, and the
moon threw open her pathway of light upon
the shining sea, as it were to bid my spirit
pass up the ladder of vision unto God.

Could I meet Him now? Was it my
destiny or my own sin that bade me despair
and die? Across that wave and sky, from
beyond the stars, I heard loving voices call
me, who had none to love me on earth,
' Leila, Leila——.' I remembered my
father's voice, unheard since early childhood,
I knew it now, deep and tender, for evermore; and a whisper came beside it, from
the mother's heart that ceased to beat when
mine began. Why were they taken and
I left in misery behind them? Yes, they
were calling me now, with clear voices
from the world of spirits—did they know
of my sorrows, and even in the mansions
of the Highest could they weep for me?
And I looked again into the far horizon of
the deep sea that separated me from the
bright distant land where their earthly
troubles slept beneath yonder light now
shining on my wretchedness alike. How
could I share their rest? I asked myself;
in what manner would death come and
take me? I felt him very near, and
trembled not. Was he coming to woo me
with a bridegroom's kiss, more faithful and
true than his which burned my brow and

lips with fire, and had left upon my soul
the ineffaceable mark of that baptism,
eternal as i's own existence? I was re-
minded of a story my ayah told me, when
I was a little child, of the lovely princess
' Krishna Kumari,' for whom the countries
of Rajpootanee were plunged in fratricidal
war by the claims of rival princes to her
hand, and how, to stay the cruel slaughter,
and give peace to the land of her birth,
the royal maid accepted the poisoned cup
tendered to her lips by her wretched
father's own hand, and, as she said ' This is
the bridegroom foredoomed for me,' drank it,
and speaking, trembled, sank down, and
died—the theme of an heroic story, early
in our nineteenth century. I fell asleep,
and dreamed I was an Indian princess, and
that a cup of poison was held before me
by an invisible hand. I bent my head
down to drink, and saw her face, my rival's,
in the bottom of the cup, as it were re-
flected in a glass—I awoke with a cry, and
saw that another day had risen on the sea.
I felt faint, and it came to my mind that I
had been wandering for a day and a night
without food. But I suffered no comm..n

hunger, the deep passion-thirst of the soul
had quenched the sense of bodily need ;
the tenderness and anguish of love came
upon me, and I moaned, a loud, wailing
note, that startled and pierced me through,
as it were some strange voice of nature's
unspeakable pangs—the sough of the wind
among the dark waves, or the murmured
moan of the troubled waters ; then the
memory of a dear voice came whispering
peace to my ear and heart, like the bird's
love-note of wooing to its mate : it could
not be denied or resisted by any strength
that was in me—I felt myself sink into his
arms to die with joy—but then—the
thought flashed upon me like lightning—
to divide his affections with her ! I spurned
the poisoned delight untasted from my lips.
Oh, God, my jealousy ! that pang was as
teeth of fire within my bosom—how had I
been infected with such horrible feelings,
as in my ignorance I dreamed not of ?
Had I fallen asleep in Paradise, after
tasting of the apple of the fall, and awaked
with ten years' sin and sorrow laid in one
night as a pall upon my young life's days ?

I thought of the Shunamite, the mystic

bride of the great king, of the pains of her bliss; was love, then, in itself a pain? What must it then be to me, deceived, betrayed, abandoned? Was there no remedy for such wretches as I? Yes, one; I thought of it now, looking upon the bright blue water, glittering in the early sunlight, cold and beautiful, and upon me the desire was very strong to allay the awful fever of the heart as 'burning Sappho' allayed it, in the old Greek days, when women loved as women can love now. I was lying upon the scanty grass mixed with sand, which made me not too smooth a couch, upon a headland, not so high, perhaps, as the rock of Leucadia, from which the Lesbian leaped down to make her eternal rest in the deep sea's bed. But I could see the waters risen to a height more than would cover my head, and roll over it, as the tide came in; and down beneath, through their clear depths, the shells and shingles and sea-ferns showed distinct and beautiful as the floor of a siren's chamber. I looked long, and with keen and piercing gaze, and a resistless impulse came upon me—I knew no more.

I was beneath the waters, shut out from
air, though not from light. I could see
and realise the horror, while I could not
breathe; my life was being torn from me
in dumb agony, all the torments of strangu-
lation were upon me. I struggled madly,
and my anguish was the more—to my
amazement, I came to the surface, and felt
the sun warm upon me, to breathe the air
I had no time. I sank again, and felt no
more pain! there were bells ringing in my
ears, and I knew they would go on until
the echo of all mortal sounds should die
out in one great silence.

I was lying in bed when I awoke to
sensation, not my own bed, as I saw very
soon. Close upon me were the narrow
walls of a cottage, a strange, but kindly
face was by my pillow—a fisherman's wife,
as I discovered afterwards ; her husband
it was who saw my cloak floating on the
water, and discovering a human being
beneath it, plunged in and rescued me in
time, from what he supposed to be an
accidental peril of drowning. As soon as
I recovered my senses, the fisher-wife
called to my poor old grandmother, whom

I had not seen at first, as she sat at the foot of my bed in silent despair. She rose, and in violent agitation, motioned the woman to leave us alone together.

'Grannie,' I said—I found I scarce could speak, 'I threw myself into the sea, to take away my own life—if I recover, Grannie, you will not say unkind things again—you will not drive me to do such an act?'

'Hush, hush! for God's sake—don't let them hear you talk so! Did you do it on purpose? Let it be thought it was an accident—think of the disgrace, the ruin to us both, if the world knew—I'll do anything you like, my darling child; only keep that unknown for ever.'

'What should you have done if I had been dead?'

'Oh, child, child! what should I do but lie down and die too?'

I was subdued by the words of kindness; I fell on her neck and kissed her, weeping aloud, while she kept crying, 'Hush, hush! —take care they don't hear.'

I clung to her now with all a daughter's love—poor old helpless thing! how wicked

and cruel it was to give her so much
harrowing anxiety ! I clasped her to my
heart as its only precious possession that
God had left, and we wept for each other :
was she not the sole frail plank between me
and utter desolation now ?

END OF VOL. I.

REMINGTON AND CO., 133, NEW BOND STREET, W.